Contents

DECONSTRUCTING PUBLIC RELATIONS

Public Relations Criticism

Thomas J. Mickey
Bridgewater State College

2003

LAWRENCE ERLBAUM ASSOCIATES, PUBLISHERS
Mahwah, New Jersey London

Lawrence Erlbaum Associates, Inc., Publishers
10 Industrial Avenue
Mahwah, NJ 07430

Cover design by Kathryn Houghtaling Lacey

Library of Congress Cataloging-in-Publication Data

Mickey, Thomas J.
Deconstructing public relations: public relations criticism / Thomas J. Mickey
p. cm.
Includes bibliographical references and index.
ISBN 0-8058-3748-5 (cloth : alk. Paper)
ISBN 0-8058-3749-3 (pbk. : alk. paper)
Public relations. 2. Deconstruction. I. Title. II. Series.
HM1221 .M52 2002
659.2—dc21

2001054848
CIP

Books published by Lawrence Erlbaum Associates are printed on acid-free paper, and their bindings are chosen for strength and durability.

Printed in the United States of America
10 9 8 7 6 5 4 3 2 1

Preface

What I try to do in this book is to show how public relations belongs to the everyday process of social construction. With all its material, public relations practice is basically a cultural product. Therefore, I believe that anyone interested in public relations should not be afraid to deconstruct public relations by challenging its assumed autonomy as a privileged mode of representation.

I have been writing about public relations as a cultural artifact for the past 10 years. This book contains much of that work, always pursuing a critical view of the field.

For my own inspiration for this book, I am grateful to a wonderful essay by J. B. Harley (1991) on deconstruction. I paraphrase his view here; where he originally talked about making maps, I substitute public relations as the practice. The interpretive act of deconstructing public relations can serve three functions. First, it allows us to challenge the epistemological myth of the cumulative progress of what many call an objective science. Second, the deconstructionist argument allows us to redefine the social importance of public relations. Third, a deconstructive turn of mind may allow public relations to take a fuller place in the interdisciplinary study of text and knowledge.

—Thomas J. Mickey
Rye, New Hampshire

ACKNOWLEDGMENTS

I first want to thank the Center for Academic Research and Teaching (CART) at Bridgewater State College, Bridgewater, MA, for a Summer Grant to work on this book. Thanks also to Patty Benson, who patiently edited and typed the final manuscript.

"Representation of Woman" (chap. 4) is from the book *Mass Communication: Mixing Views*, edited by Jabbar A. Al-Obaidi, who kindly let me use it again here. The chapter called "Selling the Internet" (chap. 5) was first published in *Public Relations Review*.

REFERENCE

Harley, J. B. (1991). Deconstructing the Map. In T. J. Barnes & J. S. Duncan (Eds.), *Writing worlds: Discourse, text, and metaphors in the representation of landscape* (pp. 231–273). London: Routledge.

CHAPTER ONE

Why Deconstruct?

The term *deconstruction* denotes reading a text in a particular kind of way that challenges its assumed meaning. Johnson (1988) noted:

> Deconstruction is not synonymous with "destruction," however. It is in fact much closer to the original meaning of the word "analysis" itself, which etymologically means "to undo"—a virtual synonym for "to de-construct." ... If anything is destroyed in a deconstructive reading, it is not the text, but the claim to unequivocal domination of one mode of signifying over another.

Even though public relations may be an important part of contemporary culture, we need to deconstruct it. Deconstructing means to see ideas that rest under the surface of the material we have produced—to peel away the layers that are in front of us but often hidden until we look. This is especially important for public relations, because its reason for being is to promote a client, an organization, a product, or a service. The question of 'why' may not enter the arena of discussion when planning public relations activities. The public relations professional does the job because he/she assumes the value of public relations; but precisely because we assume its benefit to society is reason enough for raising questions about the material practice of public relations.

Norris (1991) wrote that deconstruction starts out by rigorously suspending the assumed correspondence among mind, meaning, and the concept of method that claims to unite them.

Concepts need to be perpetually shaken and dislodged. We deconstruct something to improve it, make it more effective, and enable people to be freer by the process. Therefore, deconstruction neither denies nor really affects the commonsense view that language exists to communicate meaning. It suspends that view for its own specific purpose of seeing what happens when the writs of convention no long run (Norris, 1991).

Material practice means that what is done is constructed in the light of a particular theory. Williams said that all praxis is based on some idea or theory (1976). Public relations as a material practice means that the campaign includes empirical data that can be examined. The material may be a video, a speech, a press release, or a brochure. All of it, however, is colored by some kind of theory about values like society, self, gender, power, and race.

Deconstructing raises questions about public relations. It seeks to know why, for whose welfare, or in what other sense might we understand the material. One could deconstruct public relations in various ways. You could interview the people who produced the campaign. You could examine the material from a campaign. You could ask people for whom the campaign is developed what the campaign means to them.

In this book, we concentrate on looking at the material text of a campaign. The text becomes the focus of deconstructing. Thus, to deconstruct public relations here is to raise questions about the text.

This book seeks to reflect the work of French philosopher Jacques Derrida, who proposed that one deconstruct a text as a way of examining the ideas proposed in the text. It is completely rational to look at ideas presented to us in materials produced under the term *public relations*. Caputo (1997) maintained that every deconstructive analysis is undertaken in the name of something, something affirmatively undeconstructible. What is undeconstructible—for example, justice or democracy—is neither real nor ideal, neither present nor future-present, neither existent nor idealizable This is how and why it incites our "desire" while driving and impassioning deconstruction.

For example, Derrida stated that the law is deconstructible, because it is constructed in the first place. Such deconstructibility is not bad news; it is a way to "improve the law" (Caputo, 1997, p. 130). We can therefore never have enough of deconstruction.

Every time the law tends to fold in on itself and become legalistic, or when it is concerned more with formal legality or legitimization and rectitude than with justice, deconstruction is needed.

The work of deconstruction thus can become a critical reflection on public relations work. We question the purpose of a particular public relations project, whether employee communications, government lobbying, community relations, crisis communication, or product promotion. We look at the point of view in the campaign. We examine the data or evidence for that point of view as well as the assumptions of that view.

The reader may draw several conclusions. One might argue that deconstructing public relations means to look at public relations critically; that is, to pose questions of value for whom or for what, with whose political benefit, or with what economic pressure to bear. Paul (1993), who discussed critical thinking, pointed us in the right direction to deconstruct public relations material when he wrote that we question the ideas and assumptions in the material. By deconstructing, we apply critical thinking to public relations practice.

The concept of representation enters into deconstructing. Public relations materials have a particular view that is constructed with self-interest at heart. Any representation, however, is limited, and frequently limiting in a democratic environment. Soon, however, it often becomes part of the culture's thinking and being: We think this is the way it is when it is really one person's or one organization's view.

L'Etang and Pieczka (1996) noted that public relations practice often lacks a reflection from critical theory, Marxism, or postmodernism. Their conclusion is that public relations is usually searching for problem-solving views, and does not seem interested in a self-reflective approach that might criticize it. The approach of this book assumes a critical view through deconstruction.

A critical approach to public relations practice can stand on its own. The purpose is not necessarily to learn how to do a better campaign, although that may result. In a rational society, a critical theory—like deconstructing—is valuable in itself so that we continue to use reason and dialogue as the basis of a democratic society.

There are many examples of writers who suggest a critical look at what we assume to be accepted and unquestioned ways of functioning in the society. For example, Scott (1994) suggested the need for a theory of visual rhetoric as a way to look at examples of visual communication. Poster (1982) proposed a link between semiotics and critical theory. He asserted that one needs to look at the text, composed of signs and symbols, from a more critical theory and not simply accept signs and symbols as given.

We are less conscious, perhaps, of the degree to which we take for granted a set of public relations values that in reality are not absolute, but instead are culturally structured. To ask questions of public relations material is to deconstruct it. Therefore, a critique of certain fundamental preconceptions of the public relations view is implied in the chapters that follow.

REFERENCES

Caputo, J. (1997). (Editor). *Deconstruction in a nutshell: A conversation with Jacques Derrida*. New York: Fordham University Press.

Johnson, B. (1988). *The critical difference: Essays in the contemporary rhetoric of reading*. Baltimore, MD: John Hopkins University Press.

L'Etang, J., & Pieczka, M. (1996). *Critical perspectives in public relations*. London: International Thomson Business Press.

Norris, C. (1991). *Deconstruction: Theory and practice*. London: Routledge.

Paul, R. (1993). *Critical thinking: What every person needs to survive in a rapidly changing world*. Cotati, CA: Foundation for Critical Thinking.

Poster, M. (1982). Semiology and critical theory: From Marx to Baudrilard. In W. V. Soparos et al. (Eds.), *The questions of textuality* (pp. 275–287). Bloomington: Indiana University Press.

Scott, L. M. (1994). Images in advertising: The need for a theory of visual rhetoric. *Journal of Consumer Research, 21*, 252–273.

Williams, R. (1976). *Keywords: A vocabulary of culture and society*. Oxford, UK: Oxford University Press.

CHAPTER TWO

Cultural Studies Approach

One July afternoon, actor Danny Glover spoke to a group of African American children in Boston. His message focused on the dangers of smoking, but he also mentioned the need to stay in school in order to achieve one's goals (Kong & Vaillancourt, 1994). The ideas seemed like something the youngsters needed to hear. Glover provided the perfect role model.

The Glover event was sponsored by the R. J. Reynolds Tobacco Company as a public relations strategy. All of the Boston media covered the event. The fact that Glover was there received media attention for RJR, which needed positive public opinion.

A critical question one needs to ask is what this media event was saying about the practice of public relations. The event did not just happen, but was orchestrated by public relations counsel. Every practice in the culture, defined here as social action, needs to be open to critical inquiry, because it is a construction by actors who stand to gain something from the practice. Public relations "practice" is no exception.

The Glover appearance provided a forum for the value system of R. J. Reynolds (RJR) to receive public support. RJR is a company involved in producing a product that has long been responsible for smoke-related diseases.

Glover's talk was not just slick public relations or a good example of "spin"; rather, these questions need to be asked: What kind of political and economic environment provides the setting for such practice? Why was this strategy used? And, finally, why do some members of the audience accept a positive meaning from this personal appearance by an African American movie star? All of these questions hinge on the importance of using critical theory to examine public relations practice.

The objective of this chapter is to propose cultural studies as an approach to critical theory for public relations. Public relations exists only in practice, in what social actors do, in what has become a way to do public relations. All practices in the culture are constructions of language and symbol, and thus are representations of power.

Cultural studies—which began in Birmingham, England, during the 1950s with such writers as Raymond Williams—seeks to look at any text as a production of class, power, and oppression. It is an appropriate vehicle to examine public relations from the perspective of deconstruction.

Toth and Heath (1992) noted that critical theory in public relations ought to be confrontational. From the beginning, cultural studies writers have walked that path. Their approach is not simply to examine popular culture, as some researchers do, but also to highlight the oppression through cultural forms and even propose policy change to address that inequity.

Harms and Kellner (1991) asserted that a critical theory operates via a standpoint of human emancipation from unnecessary and unjust forms of domination. To study public relations from a critical theory perspective is to raise the social consciousness of forms of oppression. At first glance, such a task might seem difficult for a field so practical as public relations, but today it is more important and necessary than ever as the media become more and more dependent on public relations sources for news and entertainment.

In cultural studies, texts are considered a form of oppression. They represent a reality that codifies the power of a few over others in the culture. Cultural studies seeks to examine the making of meaning and the coding of value for a society. Therefore, the focus is often on what the practice or text "means" to the receiver: What scene, words, actor, and so on are in the communication form. The question is the choice of symbol or language within a certain structure or coding system.

The questions to be investigated here are: How can we critically evaluate the meaning of public relations practice for the culture? What do public relations strategies mean for the audience? What do they mean for a democratic society?

Fiske (1989) noted that culture is a struggle for meanings, just as society is a struggle for power. Therefore, to understand public relations practice is to understand the distribution of power in the culture: who has it and who doesn't.

The method here is first a literature review of critical theory in public relations. Then, we take a look at the definition and history of cultural studies as both a theory and method. Finally, the chapter concludes with a discussion of the value of the cultural studies approach as a model for public relations critical theory.

A number of articles have addressed the issue of critical theory in public relations:

- Olasky (1985) conducted a qualitative analysis of 40 years of articles appearing in the *Public Relations Journal*, but found mostly public relations for public relations when it came to questions of criticism of public relations practice from an ethical basis. Although public relations leaders may point to a number of journal articles on ethics as a sign that criticism is being taken seriously, Olasky showed the superficiality of all but a few articles on criticism of public relations.
- Pearson (1986) linked the themes in public relations literature with the critical theory of Habermas to develop criteria for evaluating public relations programming.
- Feldman (1988) examined the public relations program of the electrical industry in the 1920s. His was a critical study that employed both historical and economic data to support the argument. He made extensive use of various kinds of public relations material.
- Peterson (1988) took a critical look at the public relations materials of the Grand Teton National Park. Her work was mainly rhetorical theory used to examine organizational myth.
- Toth (1989) examined the ideology around gender in the practice of public relations. She recommended similar public relations critical research in the future. Since then, there have been several studies, including that of Creedon

(1991), who dealt with gender and public relations practice by examining salary and task inequities in the workplace.

- Badaracco (1990) took a critical stand in her view of public relations practice as a culture industry. She examined the rise of modern publicity at the turn of the century. Publicity as a business has matured since then, from a trade to a managerial activity that has become something we export more of than any tangible good but without tariff or protective barriers.
- Sriramesh (1992) looked critically at public relations practice in India. Public relations there is linked to the culture insofar as its values and ideology are both produced and supported by the kind of public relations in practice.
- Moffitt (1992) borrowed a term from cultural studies, *articulation theory*. Her critical mission here was an interpretive look at public relations, in which she argued that the "public" in public relations practice must be given a voice.
- Coffin (1994) discussed promotional material to sell sewing machines in late nineteenth-century France. Her critical look at both the public relations and the advertising as text highlighted the promotion of ideology and values like credit, consumption, and a certain image of women.
- Toth and Heath (1994) maintained that the reason for critical theory in public relations should be to disrupt our beliefs about organizations. Critical scholars of public relations often use organizational values as well as written messages as the unit of analysis when looking at the practice of public relations. Toth and Heath developed three predominant paradigms of research in public relations: social science, rhetorical, and critical. The amount of research in each area illustrates how little is devoted to critical theory: social science (70%), rhetorical (20%), and critical (10%).
- German (1995) deconstructed public relations practice. She examined the ideology and value system implicit in the public relations text.
- Millar (1995) surveyed articles in the *Journal of Public Relations Research* from 1987 to 1995. He concluded that more critical research is needed.

- McDonald (1995) did a review of the kinds of public relations articles in *Journalism Quarterly*. She concluded that public relations research is becoming diverse, but critical research is practically nonexistent. She called this an area that needed to be addressed.
- Kruckeberg (1995) pointed out the ideological basis of public relations practice that makes it culture bound. He suggested that ethics is critically important to police the inherently unethical, asymmetrical models of public relations, because such ethics establish boundaries beyond which the practice of these models should not transcend.
- Hirston-Shea and Benoit (1996) examined the public relations text of the Tobacco Institute as a response to a series of "Doonesbury" cartoons.

There is also evidence of some research on public relations from a cultural studies perspective. Following is a list of some writers who approach public relations practice as an expression of power in the culture, but a power that needs to be open to critical inquiry because of the voices that go unheard:

- Gamson (1994) took a cultural studies approach to publicity for celebrities. He wrote, "Celebrity is a never ending series of images to be read, so that even those whose truth appears to be that they are in control of their own manufacture cannot be known to be so and must also be read as essentially fictional. Reading the celebrity text from this angle is like encountering mirrors facing one another: there is no end-point, no final ground" (p. 158).
- Another approach to a critical theory reading of public relations was taken by Jeff and Marie Blyskal (1985), who sought to show how the public relations industry writes the news. This is also an example of a critical view of public relations practice and its role in the culture.
- A book by Trento (1992) critically examined the work of one of Washington D.C.'s public relations practitioners. Trento delved into the cultural significance of Robert Gray's public relations practice among the nation's corporate and political leaders.

- Stauber and Rampton's book (1996) has been hailed the best critical book on the public relations industry in recent years. Written by a pair who have no vested interest in the public relations field but do care for a democratic society, the book critiqued the public relations industry. The book featured one public relations campaign that codes toxic sludge as "good for you."
- A book by Ewen (1997) also took a cultural studies view. Ewen sought to criticize public relations because of the threat to democracy that this practice has provided since the start of the twentieth century.

The literature to date points out important issues to consider in addressing public relations theory and research. First, although there clearly exists some work from a critical perspective, there still remains a pressing need for more critical theory as applied to public relations practice. Second, the issue of ethics or social accountability of public relations is more crucial than ever. Third, there is a link between public relations practice and the production of culture. Finally, one frequent, effective method for critical research in public relations is to look at the public relations text (i.e., material produced by a public relations professional, such as press releases, brochures, speeches, etc.).

Horkheimer (1982) noted that the critical theory of society is human beings as producers of their own historical way of life in its totality. The goal of critical theory is emancipating human beings from the relationships in the culture that enslave them.

One could begin a discussion of cultural studies as critical theory by invoking the metaphor of a garden. We walk into a garden called "critical theory." Inside, we see smaller areas like the Frankfurt School, Jurgen Habermas, and feminism as separate gardens within the larger garden, each with its own design and plants. Over to the one side we see another area called *cultural studies*.

Cultural studies started in England in the 1950s. It has sprouted in many forms all around the world since then. In fact, many universities now include departments, sequences, and courses in cultural studies.

Here, we see the original spot for cultural studies in the garden of critical theory. One might term its central ideas as its seeds: The terms are *symbol, discourse, text, culture, representation*, and *hegemony*. These seeds have given us many plants, which resulted in studies in critical theory.

The original ideas or seeds centered on how culture, through its symbols (primarily media) exerts control and power, and how it privileges some members of the culture over others. The high/low culture debate became important to cultural studies researchers and continues to be important today. The low culture looks at the same media as the high, and aspires to be like the high in that gaze. For example, a middle-class homeowner may exhibit a copy of the *New Yorker* on the coffee table at home, so that visitors will be impressed with his/her class aspiration.

The focus on the discourse of literature and media gave cultural studies its material basis in the "text": It looks at the development of culture as the expression of the dominant texts. Thus, novels in the nineteenth century were viewed as being low class, much like television in the 1950s was viewed as being low class. Today, those same novels are considered important reading for the "cultured" person.

The text can be looked at from its *production* by communication professionals like journalists and writers, and also from the view of its *consumption* by the audience. Who decides on the words, music, and imagery in the text? How is it promoted and disseminated in the culture? Finally, how does the audience member consume the product? All of these questions are critical to understanding the meaning of the text for the culture.

The text is understood as an expression of political and economic power. Therefore, the discussion of context always becomes crucial when critiquing the text. Every symbol represented in the text promotes a certain ideology. Thus, in cultural studies, it is not just a matter of looking at the text but also of asking the question of whose power is being promoted at whose expense.

Social practices form a way to understand the culture and are representations constructed by actors in the culture. For example, how to spend a vacation or how to celebrate Thanksgiving carry certain practices with them in our culture.

Ideology is always represented to the culture. A writer or producer decides something is important to say and presents it or codes it as he/she thinks the audience will accept it. All ideas are material when coded as representations of age, gender, occupation, health, and so on in a product like a public service announcement, a press release, or a speech.

Hegemony means the promotion of a dominant ideology or voice in the culture. The dominant ideology tends to repeat its message in various forms. Thus, for example, skinheads may be featured as "freaks" on TV talk shows, in newsmagazines, and in the popular press.

The approach of cultural studies is critical insofar as it points out the voice that is disenfranchised. More than simply pointing out, however, it also seeks to propose ways in which that voice might be heard. Therefore, it is critical of the dominant symbol makers in the culture, especially those who—like public relations professionals—provide messages through the media.

Cultural studies first developed as a response to the social repression of the Industrial Revolution and later in response to the conservative leadership of Margaret Thatcher in England. In looking at the literature on cultural studies from England, two important names surface: Raymond Williams and Stuart Hall. Williams recognized culture as a set of specialized practices. He noticed a crisis of community in modern society, as did John Dewey much earlier in the twentieth century. Thus, Williams' roots for cultural studies are grounded in the political. Hall works within both Marxist and semiotic discourses, which attempt to understand the nature of contemporary social life and the central place of communication within it.

Few people working in cultural studies would agree on a definition, and many who claim to "do" cultural studies might not recognize themselves in the definition (Grossberg, 1997). Therefore, it is important to keep in mind that there is no one definition of cultural studies. To build an approach to public relations critical theory, we simply look at the *key terms* of cultural studies.

First, cultural studies is concerned with cultural *practices* (or *texts*), but only as a way into the context of the unequal relations of force and power in the culture. The relationship between a text or commodity and the culture is therefore important. *Culture* is the site of the production and struggle over power, where *power* is understood not necessarily in the form of domination, but always as an unequal relation of forces, in the interests of particular factions in the population. Culture is more than just a process, because it involves struggles between competing sets of practices and relations, and is thus inevitably tied up with relations of power. Culture is a site of struggle for one power's voice over another.

The politics of marginality continues to direct much of the current work in cultural studies (Grossberg, 1996). Groups that one might recognize as marginal are women, African Americans, and gays. Hence, we find studies in such areas as *gender issues* and *gay identity* that exemplify the struggle of the silenced voice.

At the heart of contemporary critical theory is the recognition that experience itself is a product of power and, therefore, that which is the most obvious, the most unquestionable, is often the most saturated by relations of power. Power is articulated by structures of difference in the culture

Cultural studies is interventionist in the sense that it attempts to use the best intellectual resources available to gain a better understanding of the relations of power in a particular context, believing that such knowledge will better enable people to change the context and hence the relations of power. Consequently, its project is always political and always partisan, but its politics are always contextually defined.

The link between context and theory defines the possibilities of cultural studies. The researcher needs to look at the historical context of the cultural practice or text. The practice of cultural studies is therefore radically contextualist, and cultural studies might be described as a discipline of contextuality. An event, practice, or a text does not exist apart from the forces of the context that constitute it as what it is. This is why larger questions of political economy become crucial when proposing to examine a cultural phenomenon from the cultural studies perspective.

The goal of cultural studies is to recast the existing social order in favor of the *silent voice*; it is not simply a look at the cultural artifacts for their own sake. We struggle between different articulations of reality to find one that is more humane for more people. Cultural studies is about the possibilities for remaking the context where context is always understood as a structure of power (Grossberg, 1997).

The objective of this chapter is to propose cultural studies as a critical theory option for the deconstruction of public relations as a cultural practice. The cultural studies approach focuses on both practice and text. The practice could, for example, be *internal*, which is the case when one needs to produce and send a message to an employee public; or it could be *external*, as when one uses the media to attract wider attention. The text could be the meaning that a word, image, or event provides for the culture. The text is always examined within a context of the economic and political arena.

As an accepted practice in planned communication whose objective is to influence others, public relations has become a way of life for the contemporary world. There seems to be no going back to a quieter time when we had fewer people calling us to join their cause or consider buying their product or service. Therefore, there ought to be an intellectual openness to criticism of this practice in a democratic society. A critical view can lead to policy change. If this openness does not come from the academic community, from where will it come? Perhaps public pressure could provide the impetus, but probably it would not come from the public relations practitioner.

The issue of ethics, often raised by public relations practitioners, will continue to be an important concern for the field, but here the critical question is much wider. Critical theory looks at the practice of public relations in the context of the capitalist system. Questions come from that basis, which may or may not imply simply following ethical guidelines as one goes about doing public relations in daily business.

A critical theory for public relations ought to give us more than hints on how to improve a campaign or how to make it more acceptable to the public. Critical theory raises questions about the values and ideology of the public relations text and thus about public relations practice itself.

Mueller (1995) wrote that all communication research ought to have some public policy implications. We ought not do research for its own sake. Mueller stipulated that communication scholarship has not played a prominent role in defining the way changes in institutions and larger society are understood.

Cultural studies could give public relations practice an opportunity for self-examination that might have an impact on the larger society. For example, public relations critical theory based on a deconstructive or cultural studies approach could look at video news releases or even truth in advertising as applied to public relations material.

Public relations critical researchers may help the democratic process by deconstructing the text of public relations communications. Therefore, any cultural studies research ought to be rooted in political and economic issues that can provide access to a silent voice or a disenfranchised minority. The field of public relations can only stand to benefit from applying the approach of cultural studies as a critical theory.

It is clear that much of the research and theory in the field of public relations is based on social science and rhetoric, but public relations is too important a phenomenon in society to limit the approach to understanding its meaning for the culture. There is a need to be aware of how our choices of word and image validate power and meaning for the culture.

Public relations is a cultural practice. As such, it needs to be viewed in terms of its relationship to the culture from a critical perspective for the purpose of human emancipation.

Cultural studies is both a theory and a method to explore a text produced by the culture in terms of its political meaning for the culture. Each text represents an articulation of power. It is important that we know who has power in the culture and who does not. Such understanding may open the door for social action and policy change, and thus greater democratization of society, all of which could be the goals for critical cultural studies and deconstruction.

Turow (1995) suggested that rather than tying most of its research into social psychology and intra-organizational communication, future public relations research ought to look into history, political science, sociology, and cultural studies. He challenged those who know the public relations industry and have vested interest in it to be at the forefront of applying critical theory to the practice.

There is much research in public relations at the moment, but too little in the area of critical theory. The field of public relations practice needs to consider the resources of the cultural studies tradition in its own self-reflection and in its current need for more critical public relations work.

REFERENCES

Badaracco, C. (1990). Publicity and modern influence. *Public Relations Review, 16*(3), 5–18.

Blyskal, J., & Blyskal, M. (1985). *PR: How the public relations industry writes the news*. New York: Morrow.

Coffin, J. G. (1994). Credit, consumption, and images of women's desires: Selling the sewing machine in late nineteenth century France. *Journal of French Historical Studies, 18*, 749–783.

Creedon, P. (1991). Public relations and "Women's Work", Toward a feminist analysis of public relations roles. In L. A. Grunig & J. E. Grunig (Eds.), *Public relations research annual* (pp. 67–84). Hillsdale, NJ: Lawrence Erlbaum Associates.

Ewen, S. (1997). *PR!: A social history of spin*. New York: Basic Books.

Feldman, A. (1988). *Selling the "electrical dream" in the 1920's: A case study in the manipulation of consciousness*. Paper presented at the Annual Meeting of the Association for Education in Journalism and Mass Communication, Portland, OR. July.

Fiske, J. (1988). *Television culture* New York: Routledge.

Gamson, J. (1994). *Claims to fame: Celebrity in contemporary America*. Berkeley: University of California Press.

German, K. (1995). Critical theory in public relations inquiry. In W. N. Elwood (Ed.), *Public relations as rhetorical criticism* (pp. 279–294). Westport, CT: Praeger.

Grossberg, L. (1996). History, politics, and postmodernism: Stuart Hall and cultural studies. In D. Morley & K.-H. Chen (Eds.), *Stuart Hall: Critical dialogues in cultural studies* (pp. 151–173). Westport, CT: Praeger.

Grossberg, L (1997). *Bringing it all back home: Essays on cultural studies*. Durham, NC: Duke University Press.

Harms, J., & Kellner, D. (1991). Critical theory and advertising. *Current Perspectives in Social Theory, 11*, 41–67.

Hirston-Shea, D., & Benoit, W. L. (1996). *Doonesbury versus the tobacco industry*. Paper presented at the Annual Meeting of the Speech Communication Association, San Diego, CA.

Horkheimer, M. (1982). *Critical theory*. New York: Seabury.

Johnson, R. (1986–87). What is cultural studies anyway? *Social Text, 16*, 38–80.

Kong, D., & Vaillancourt, M. (1994, July 16). Smoking foes blast actor's appearance at school. *Boston Globe*, p. 20.

Kruckeberg, D. (1995). *A global perspective on public relations ethics: The Middle East*. Paper presented at the Annual Meeting of the Speech Communication Association, San Antonio, TX.

McDonald, B. (1995). *What current research tells us about public relations*. Paper presented at the Annual Meeting of the Speech Communication Association, San Antonio, TX.

Millar, D. (1995). *What current research tells us about public relations*. Paper presented at the Annual Meeting of the Speech Communication Association, San Antonio, TX.

Moffitt, M. A. (1992). Bringing critical theory and ethical considerations to definitions of a "public." *Public Relations Review, 18*(1), 17–30.

Mueller, M. (1995). Why communications policy is passing "mass communication" by: Political economy as the missing link. *Critical Studies in Mass Communication, 12*(4), 457–472.

Olasky, M. (1985). How the public relations journal responds to criticism of public relations ethics: A qualitative approach (Eric Document: ED258263).

Pearson, R. (1986). *The ideal public relations situation: Alternative criteria for program evaluation*. Paper presented at the Annual Meeting of the Association for Education in Journalism and Mass Communication, Norman, OK.

Peterson, T. R. (1988). The meek shall inherit the mountains: A dramatistic criticism of Grand Teton National Park's interpretive program. *Central States Speech Journal, 39*(2), 121–133.

Sriramesh, K. (1992). Societal culture and public relations: Ethnographic evidence from India. *Public Relations Review, 18*(2), 201–211.

Stauber, J., & Rampton, S. (1996). *Toxic sludge is good for you*. Monroe, ME: Common Courage Press.

Toth, E. (1989). *Whose freedom and equity in public relations? The gender balance argument*. Paper presented at the Annual Meeting of the Association for Education in Journalism and Mass Communication, Washington, DC.

Toth, E., & Heath, R. (Eds.). (1992). *Rhetorical and Critical approaches to public relations*. Hillsdale, NJ: Lawrence Erlbaum Associates.

Trento, S. (1992). *Power house: Robert Keith Gray and the selling of access and influence in Washington*. New York: St. Martin's Press,

Turow, J. (1995, Autumn). Book review of *Public Relations Research Annual*, Volume 3. *Journal of Communication*, pp. 178–180.

CHAPTER THREE

Alcohol as Medicine

This chapter examines the relationship between promotional language and power. Promotional language refers to the language of public relations strategies. The objective of much public relations practice is often to inform the public about a product so that people will purchase it (Wilcox, Alt, & Agee, 1995). The question of power focuses on the influence that symbol makers like public relations practitioners have in a culture through word and image.

The goal of this chapter is to present a social history of the promotion of a Pabst Brewing Company product called Tonic, which was bottled and sold from 1888 to 1956. In the campaign, the promotional language informed the public about the beverage, maintained favorable opinion about the product, and even motivated consumers to purchase the product. What makes this case so important to the social history of public relations is that the product had as much alcohol as beer but was called a medicine.

The problem to be studied is how an industry defines a health-related product for the consumer. In this case, the medical community and the government cooperated. The industry was the Pabst Brewery in Milwaukee and the product was "Best" Tonic, sold as a medicinal food. Tonic was sold in pharmacies from 1888 to 1956, although after Prohibition and in later years it was marketed primarily outside the United States. Even during Prohibition (1920–1933) it was sold whenever a doctor prescribed the product for a patient.

The purpose of this chapter is to understand public relations practice as a cultural phenomenon that espouses the values of a group at a particular time through the construction of a text. The text here is "Best" Tonic, produced in word and image as a medicine. The major research question is to understand how the text—Pabst "Best" Tonic—was produced, distributed, and used during the late nineteenth and early twentieth centuries. A minor research question is how the medical community, especially pharmacists and the government, aided Pabst in coding the product as a medicinal food.

In a capitalist culture a product is defined by various actors in the process, and the consumer accepts that meaning, frequently without questioning. Is it possible that a product could harm the consumer? In recent times that has happened, with the tragic stories about the risks of breast implants for women.

Toth and Heath (1992) encouraged more studies based on a critical approach to the study of public relations. Cultural studies assumes the critical approach while at the same time pointing out the inequalities in the social system in which the capitalist voice often dictates values for the culture while intentionally ignoring a minority voice. This is especially evident in the media (Williams, 1974). Because product promotion relies heavily on the media, one can say it is also the case with public relations practice when the strategy involves product promotion.

The focus here is to deconstruct public relations by examining the values and ideology of public relations practice. To do that, we look at the campaign for "Best" Tonic from a cultural studies perspective.

The availability of significant primary sources makes this project feasible. The historical material comes from the archives of the Milwaukee County Historical Society, the Wisconsin Historical Association, and the American Institute of the History of the Pharmacy in Madison, Wisconsin. The Pabst Brewery has turned over its archives to the Milwaukee Historical Society. That collection, which dates back to the mid-nineteenth century, includes a substantial amount of promotional material along with records and correspondence. The Kremers Library at the American Institute of the History of Pharmacy houses a collection of letters, journals, ads, booklets, and government documents about the pharmacy industry from colonial times to the present. The Wisconsin Historical Association at the University of Wisconsin in Madison has a collection of pharmacy records from the late 1800s that includes prescription books, logs, diaries, and letters.

The history of modern public relations in the United States began in the late nineteenth century, largely due to industrialization, which resulted in numerous newspapers and consumer magazines. At that time, beer was the biggest industry in Milwaukee. Industrialization also provided the technology for large-scale brewing and bottling facilities. The breweries often highlighted the new scientific and technological advances in their facility when they promoted their beer products. One example is from the Schlitz Brewery, which sponsored an opera in Milwaukee in 1890. The printed program included the following words: "A model establishment; equipped with every appliance that modern science can suggest, skilled and experienced brewers, and above all, an unwavering adherence to its cardinal rule to employ ever and only, the best material, regardless of cost, the Schlitz Brewing Company is enabled to furnish its patrons with a pure and perfect article."[1]

Milwaukee's Pabst Brewery, created in 1844, was one of the largest in the city. Pabst was the first brewer to advertise nationally.[2] Although all the breweries depended on advertising and public relations to sell their products, promotion was the key to Pabst's great period of expansion, from 1873 to 1893 (Still, 1948). In the 1890s the Pabst Brewery employed J. Walter Thompson to promote "Best" Tonic (Downard, 1980).

Wernick (1991) discussed promotional culture as a way to understand society, maintaining that it is the language of advertising, marketing, and public relations that give us an insight into the values and ideology of the culture. Williams (1993) noted that it is impossible to look at modern advertising without realizing that the material object being sold is never enough. This indeed is the crucial quality of advertising's modern forms: The objects to be sold are not themselves enough but must be validated, if only in fantasy, by association with social and personal meanings. As well, the issue with "Best" Tonic is the social meanings that the product has for the culture: meanings produced by the brewery and the medical community, distributed by both, and subsequently consumed by patrons who wanted the product because it was a medicine.

Although promoting beer products was the goal of the Pabst public relations campaign, in studying culture it is also important to make sense of any facts presented as historical data. Because this research is grounded in public relations social history, an appropriate communication theory is important. Any research in communication is a project that needs to be rooted in some theoretical perspective.

The postmodernist thinker, Pierre Bourdieu, provided the theoretical framework for making sense of the historical data for this research. Rather than simply reporting interesting historical facts, the objective of this chapter is to use a theory to help us understand the facts from a critical perspective. Postman (1994) wrote that whatever events may be included in studies of the past, the worst thing we can do is to present them devoid of the coherence that a theory or theories can provide—that is to say, as meaningless. Bourdieu (1991) shared a similar opinion: "Every theory, as the word itself suggests, is a program of perception, but that is all the more true of theories about the social world. It seems impossible to present historical data without some underlying perspective for them" (p. 128).

Bourdieu proposed to look at language as a way of establishing power and capital in a particular culture. The language is part of the habitus of that time and period. Although many others have had similar ideas, Bourdieu developed the concept that the language used in society reinforces what is powerful in that society. When a company calls a product by a certain name, and that company has the money and support of groups significant in the culture, society accepts the product's name as reality. Therefore, one might project that when Pabst called "Best" Tonic a medicinal food, the public believed and accepted the reality of that claim because the powerful Pabst company called it so. Here is an ad that Pabst ran in 1917 about "Best" Tonic: "While made principally from malt and hops and greatly resembling in both taste and appearance dark beer or porter, Pabst Extract, The "Best" Tonic, differs materially from either of these beverages owing to its being brewed **from a medicinal standpoint** and is highly recommended by leading physicians as a Tonic of great value."[3] (emphasis added) What Pabst was saying is that because they called the Tonic medicine or medicinal, therefore it was—the name they gave it was what it was. Pabst, along with other actors like pharmacists, nurses, and doctors, defined the meaning of Tonic.

Bourdieu cautioned against looking at language or words in isolation or, as he said, in structure without looking at the function they play in society. We need to move beyond semiotics and look at the social and historical framework in which the language takes shape. What creates the power of words and slogans—a power capable of maintaining or subverting the social order—is the belief in the legitimacy of words and of those who utter them.

Bourdieu discussed the practice of symbol making in the culture, particularly the acts of political figures that we employ here to also include corporate giants like Milwaukee's Pabst Brewing Company. At the risk of unwittingly assuming responsibility for the acts of constitution of whose logic and necessity they are unaware, the social sciences must take as their object of study the social operations of *naming* and the rites of institution through which they are accomplished.

Mintz (1983) noted that culture must be approached as a complex social and cultural phenomenon—as one that must be treated as a process involving the production, distribution, and use of whatever product which is the text or artifact. Fine (1977) seemed to echo Bourdieu when he asserted, "Much can be learned about the production, consumption, and usage of popular culture, particularly if these elements are analyzed in terms of their role within social interaction. To produce any substantial cultural product a collection of individuals must combine to execute the creator's original conception" (p. 463). The cooperation of other significant groups in the culture was necessary for "Best" Tonic to continue to be sold for over 30 years.

Thompson, in the introduction to Bourdieu (1991), said:

> It is clear that Bourdieu has outlined a distinctive approach to political phenomena, an approach which has definite methodological implications. One such implication is that it would be superficial (at best) to try to analyze political discourses or ideologies by focusing on the utterances as such, without reference to the constitution of the political field and the relation between this field and the broader space **of social positions and processes**. This kind of "internal analysis" is commonplace in the academic literature, as exemplified by the numerous and varied attempts to apply some form of semiotics or "discourse

> analysis" to political speeches. The difficulty with all such attempts is similar to the difficulty that vitiates all "formalist" approaches to language (or, indeed, all purely "literary" approaches to literature): they take for granted but fail to take account of the social-historical conditions within which the object of analysis is produced, constructed, and received. (pp. 28 and 29, emphasis added)

A cultural study of deconstruction is appropriate for public relations research because there is a tradition of critical, cultural studies already present in the field. Hon (1993) proposed a feminist theory for public relations to understand the culture's devaluation of women and women's work and looked at public relations practice in relationship to the culture. The meanings produced are understood and critiqued as cultural artifacts. Those meanings cannot be accepted if women are to rise in management, increase their salaries, or achieve personal fulfillment in the field of public relations. Moral outrage in public relations practice can come from opening the door to a cultural studies approach to critical theory.

However, one cannot propose a cultural studies project without mentioning the importance of situating the text for the study. Min (1992) challenged the researcher to look at social critical theory when embarking on a cultural studies project. He recommended Bourdieu's social theory, especially the analysis of the relations between economic capital and cultural capital, as one way of providing a political and economic context for cultural studies.

Kellner (1995) called for the incorporation of new cultural theories as part of the practice of the Frankfurt School and the Birmingham tradition of cultural studies. There is a need for critical social theory to interpret, contextualize, and provide grounds to critique the findings of empirical and historical research.

Although the immediate concern here is the field of public relations, one could look at public relations as part of the tradition of communication, which, in turn, in the Frankfurt and Birmingham Schools takes on a critical perspective of the artifacts that come from culture industries like movies and newspapers. In a larger sense, one might argue that producing Tonic as a medicine was indeed an artifact of a culture industry called the public relations department of the Pabst Brewery. The distribution and the use of Tonic artifacts become important in an ideological critique and essential in a cultural studies analysis.

Much cultural studies research centers on the text, but with little reference to the social history of production or the audience use of the product (Kellner, 1995). Yet a social, economic, and political critique needs to incorporate all three avenues: production, distribution, and use. Focusing on texts and audiences to the exclusion of an analysis of the social relations and institutions in which texts are produced and consumed truncates cultural studies, as does an analysis of reception that fails to indicate how audiences are produced through their social relations and how, to some extent, culture itself helps produce audiences and their reception of texts (Kellner, 1995). In late nineteenth-century Milwaukee, the new market for beer, which was women, was the audience for whom "Best" Tonic was produced.

The method used here is textual analysis, which is one approach to doing cultural studies. Curtin (1995) discussed textual analysis as being distinct from both content analysis and discourse analysis. Textual analysis may involve looking at the meaning of the media of communication, which might include letters and journals, as well as mass-media products. "Best" Tonic promotional materials thus become the text. Coffin (1994) showed the relationship between the coding and selling of sewing machines. Images of women in the promotional materials, accompanied by a discussion of women's consumption habits, define the textual analysis of her study from nineteenth-century France.

In a cultural analysis of Channel One, Apple (1992) showed the ideology and audiences produced by such programming in building a coalition favoring the business agenda in schools. He examined news programming as the text to point out the ideology and the audience produced by that text.

Miller (1991) took a cultural studies view of advertising for suburban women from 1910 to the Depression, by pointing out the interplay among the ads, ideology, and the daily life of the consumer.

Tourism is a secular ritual in the work of Hummon (1988). The symbolic presentation of travel was documented through a textual analysis of promotional brochures and tourists for spots across the United States.

The major research question here is: How was Tonic produced, distributed, and consumed? In the tradition of cultural studies, Pabst could be considered a culture industry, and the cultural artifact that the industry produced was its Tonic, as manufactured by the brewery from 1888 to 1956.

The following terms need to be defined from Bourdieu: *capital, habitus, power,* and *language*. Bourdieu borrowed economic terms to describe society. He treated all types of practice as examples of economic transaction. The terms important to this chapter are as follows:

- *Capital*—The social influence, greater or lesser, exerted over others. The more linguistic capital there is, the more one can exploit others through words.
- *Habitus*—Individuals are already predisposed to act in certain ways, pursue certain goals, avow certain tastes, and so on.
- *Power*—Influence transmitted in symbolic form, and thereby endowed with a kind of legitimacy. Involves active complicity on the part of all the actors engaged.
- *Language*—Linguistic utterances or expressions are forms of practice. Language gets its value from the context or market in which it is produced.

Here, the text is defined as Pabst "Best" Tonic promotional material. The purpose is to understand the historical materials while using the theory of Bourdieu to interpret them. There are two parts to the following section: First, the historical data about Tonic is discussed—how the text was produced, how it was distributed, and how it was consumed; second, an interpretation of the historical material follows.

Production means how the groups and institutions put the message together. For this discussion, the primary sources include the Pabst Brewery promotional materials, correspondence, and newspaper articles. Also, the researcher conducted an interview with the Pabst historian at the company.

Distribution refers to how the message from the organization got out to the public. This material includes the label on the Tonic bottle, the publicity campaigns, ads, letters to pharmacists, drugstore window displays, special promotional books, booklets, speeches, contests, pictures, calendars, postcards, church bulletins, library slips, and streetcar posters.

Among the issues considered under consumption is how the audience used the text from the organization. That material includes articles in medical journals; letters from pharmacists, doctors, nurses, and other customers; entries in pharmacy journals and daybooks; letters to the editor; newspaper editorial content; pharmacy reference books; early twentieth-century books on pharmacy arrangement and management; and city directories.

Pabst "Best" Tonic was a malt extract drink similar to what other beverage companies offered at the end of the nineteenth century. One group, of which Trommer's or Maltine were examples, consisted of thick syrups medicated with iron, quinine, strychnine, or cod-liver oil that were taken by the spoonful. Another group, like Hoff's or Wyeth's, was made up merely of heavy-bodied, dark brews, like porter or stout, that were consumed by the glass. A bottle a day was usually recommended for improving the digestion, adding weight, or increasing energy (Cochran, 1948).

Anheuser-Busch had a product called Malt-Nutrine, a food tonic. Eisner and Mendelson of New York offered Johann Hoff's Malt Extract, which was promoted as aiding proper assimilation of food. In 1901, Hoff's was advertised in a cooking magazine called *What-To-Eat*.[4]

Pabst "Best" claimed it was the best and most advertised tonic. There is an important note of history in the title of the product. Pabst was known as the Philip Best Brewery until 1889. Tonic was first introduced in 1888, shortly before Philip Best became known as Pabst. This Best was both a reference to the earlier brewery and a pledge of quality.

By the end of the nineteenth century, brewing beer was the most important industry in Milwaukee. Beer making had been experiencing growth for 50 years. This was, to a considerable extent, the result of broadened financial foundations, new processes of manufacture, the exploitation of wider markets, and recourse to the high-powered techniques of product promotional strategies. From 1873 to 1893 the Pabst Brewing Company of Milwaukee was the nation's number one beer producer (Still, 1948).

The Pabst Brewery had its own office for promoting Tonic. In 1894, the supremacy of the product was attributed to the energetic efforts of the company to make the product known[5]: "So large have become their advertising efforts that the United States Government, at certain times of the year, established a post office for the use of the 'Best' Tonic business alone, and the volume of correspondence would be amazing to the uninitiated."[6] The Pabst Tonic Department had its own address in Milwaukee. Its first Advertising Director was George H. Yenowine, a former editor of *Yenowine's News*. Then came A. Cressy Morrison, who took over in 1889 when Yenowine resigned (Cochran, 1948).

In 1911, the Charles H. Fuller Company, an ad agency in Chicago that represented Best Tonic, sent the following letter to certain newspaper editors to promote a calendar for the product, sometimes called the Pabst Extract:

> The Pabst Extract Calendar has established a place for itself in many thousands of homes, and year after year the announcement of its publication is eagerly awaited by hundreds of subscribers. We have requested the Pabst Brewing Co. to send you a complimentary copy of the 1912 American Girl Calendar and you will no doubt agree that is the "best yet." May we ask that you favor the Pabst Brewing Co. by inserting the attached notice in your columns? We believe that your compliance with this request will not only be much appreciated by both the Pabst Brewing Co. and this agency, but also by a large number of the readers of your paper.[7]

A letter addressed to the brewery by a Chicago publishing firm and dated November 15, 1887, read as follows: "In consideration of your giving us an ad of a page in our Journal for one year, for which you are to pay $225, we will take 100 cases of the Malt Tonic and will push the sale of this article to the best of our ability. You are also to have liberty at any time to use our editorial columns regarding the merits of your malt tonic."[8]

In a promotional brochure to druggists in the 1890s, Pabst noted that a poor proprietary article or a cheap proprietary article that had no advertising margin could not live because no permanent demand for it could be created: "You know this. Our product is acknowledged to be A 1. We are the only proprietor who absolutely guarantees that he will take the goods off the druggist's shelf and give his money back. Our advertising efforts make the article 'a good seller.'"[9] Best Tonic soon also had advertising offices in Chicago and New York. At the time, it was the most highly advertised tonic in the country.[10]

What exactly was the makeup of the product called Pabst "Best" Tonic? At times it was called malt extract, a medicinal food, and a proprietary medicine. That the product had as much alcohol as beer was not mentioned very often. Two independent chemical analyses of the product appeared about 1887, which was just before the product was introduced nationally. The first test was by E. T. Fristore, a professor of Chemistry at Columbia, who measured the alcohol content at 4.49%. The second test, by E. G. Love, Ph.D., showed the alcohol content at 4.714%.[11]

In 1902, Pabst wrote a brochure defending the medicinal importance of Tonic: "It–is–not–beer. For Instance, Tokay and Malaya contain seven to fourteen per cent Alcohol; The "Best" Tonic **four and five-tenths** per cent; just the right quantity to carry with it the highest nutritive and strengthening effects. Pabst Malt Extract is a food."[12] (emphasis added)

The Tonic was also compared to a type of beer called Porter. In 1917, an ad in *Commercial America* said, "While made principally from malt and hops and greatly resembling in both taste and appearance dark beer or porter, Pabst Extract, The 'Best' Tonic, differs materially from either of these beverages owing to its being brewed from a medicinal standpoint and is highly recommended by leading physicians as a Tonic of the greatest value. Pabst Extract is not only a tonic, but a liquid food."[13]

An ad for Johann Hoff's Malt Extract in 1902 read: "Any sort of beer was called 'Malt Extract.' The market was flooded with cheap, impure, unworthy Malt Extracts."[14]

Today, Commonwealth Brewery in Boston makes a beer called Famous Porter and, according to the brewmeister, the alcohol is 5% per volume.[15] Most lagers are light in color, with high carbonation, medium hop flavor, and alcohol content of 3% to 5 % by volume. They include Pilsner, Dortmund, Munich, and California steam beer. Top-fermented beers, which are popular in Great Britain, include ale, stout, and a brew intermediate between the two, called porter. They have a sharper, more strongly hopped flavor than do lagers, and alcohol content ranging from a 4% to 6.5% or more by volume.[16] Therefore, one can say that the Pabst Brewery was selling a beer product called Tonic, because the alcohol content was almost 5%.

What is malt extract? A booklet published by Pabst circa 1900 defined it: "Malt is barley which has been allowed to sprout. By sprouting all the starch the barley is changed into food. Hops added to this food helps with sleep, serves as a nerve-tonic, and aids digestion. A liquid extracted from these two simple, pure vegetable growths is a malt extract."[17]

The bottle label clearly spelled out that the liquid extract of malt and hops was manufactured and produced by the Pabst Brewing Company. The recommended dosage was a wineglass at each meal and one before retiring, which equaled one bottle each day. It was common to promote purchasing a case of the product rather than just a bottle.

One frequent validation for the product was based on the award it received at the World's Colombian Exposition in Chicago on May 17, 1894. "Best" received the highest score possible. Table 3.1 shows the categories for judging the tonic and the perfect score that Pabst won.

That it was recognized by the Exposition was important for Pabst Tonic promotion, because no other tonic could make such a claim. The ad in which the Award was detailed used these words: "This extract of malt is more of a medicinal product than a beverage."[18] The Exposition recognized the product as a medicine.

The government gave its approval to the product as well. In an ad from Pabst dated 1914, this line appeared: "The United States Government specially classifies Pabst Extract as an article of medi-

TABLE 3.1

Category	*Maximum Points*	*Points Received*
Brilliancy	15	15
Flavor	20	20
Commercial importance	20	20
Chemical analysis	45	45
Total:	**100**	**100**

cine—not an alcoholic beverage."[19] This is based on a letter Pabst sent to the government indicating that the beverage was a medicine and was being sold as such. The government confirmed that in a letter dated May 12, 1908.

Thereafter, the Pabst Tonic stationery from the Milwaukee office of the brewery had these words at the top: "Guaranteed under the Food and Drugs Act June 30, 1906. Serial No. 1921."[20] There was no direct reference to "Best" Tonic in the act; instead, there was simply a letter from the government (quoted earlier) saying that the product was recognized at that time as a medical product as long as it was sold as such. It appears that Pabst had some promotional leverage through this government response, which almost took on the character of a government endorsement for the product.

The campaign in consumer magazines was national. Pabst said, "Our newspaper advertising is read by over seven million people. Our magazine advertising goes to over six and a half million homes every month."[21] Some of the magazines were *American Sunday Monthly, Associated Sunday Magazine, Ladies World, Pictorial Review, Dressmaking at Home, American Magazine, Cosmopolitan*, and *Harper's Bazaar.* The heading of some of the ads read as follows: "Insure Baby's Health and Vigor," "Health and Beauty," "Aged but Active," "Motherhood," "Insomnia," "Approaching Motherhood," "Convalescence," and "Nervousness."

Pabst also undertook a separate campaign for its Tonic to medical journals. The journals included *American Journal of Clinical Medicine, Chicago Medical Recorder, Medical Council, Medical World, Pediatrics*, and *Trained Nurse*. The ads featured such themes as convalescents, approaching motherhood, sound sleep, nursing mothers, old age, and anemia.[22]

Just before he resigned from Pabst, Yenowine had started publishing the Secret Booklet series, which were small booklets, about the size of a postcard, with 25–50 thin pages of riddles and jokes. This series was designed for amusement and contained little direct advertising, although the fact that 37,000,000 were distributed in just a couple of years was an argument for the value of "Best" Tonic (Cochran, 1948). The names of the booklets were *Untold Secrets, Wedding Secrets, Home Secrets, Baby Secrets*, and *Ominous Secrets*. The 50th anniversary booklet from Pabst claimed that the "Secret" books were so well known because there were more in circulation than any other book published except the Bible.[23]

Pabst edited a special book for nurses, with tips and suggestions for their work. In it was a pitch for using Tonic when the case required that a patient get rest, build a stronger constitution, or overcome nervousness.

The elderly became a target audience for the product as well. One of the Tonic ads featured these words: "Take a new lease on life—banish the ills of old age. The soothing and toning properties of hops, blended with the rich, nourishing extract of barley malt, furnish an ideal combination for building-up and strengthening the wasted tissues of the body."

Another flyer from the company said: "Every family should have a dozen bottles in the cellar to use as needed for all kinds of nervousness, loss of sleep, poor appetite or impaired digestion. It is also especially good for nursing mothers and for aged and infirm persons."[24]

A red, white, and blue 1909 ad for "Best" Tonic read: "Pabst Extract, the 'Best' Tonic for the old folks." The image used was a white-bearded old man pouring some tonic for an elderly white-haired woman sitting in a chair.[25]

Water was not fit to drink at the time. Milk was not pasteurized. With a harangue against tea as a beverage, Pabst proposed that women workers drink "Best" Tonic: "Stenographers, teachers, nurses, try a glassful at bedtime, and enjoy girlhood's untroubled sleep again."

Pregnant women were encouraged to take Tonic. Busy housewives who might get nervous and have trouble sleeping were encouraged to take Tonic. One ad showed a well-dressed woman at a druggist's counter, eyeing a case of Tonic. Because saloons were male bastions, women were the market for Tonic, which they could buy in their local drugstore. In ledger entries for Kopf Pharmacy in Milwaukee, dated October 21 and 24, 1897, we read that Mrs. A. Rhoda purchased "Best" Tonic at 25 cents per bottle.[26]

An ad in *Dressmaking at Home* in 1910 read: "Perfect happiness always is perfect health. Build up those wasted tissues—infuse new life into your blood—reconstruct worn out nerve cells and fit yourself to enjoy the vigor and energy of youth. Keep yourself in trim with a little of Pabst Extract The 'Best' Tonic each day. It is a pure, wholesome, predigested liquid food."[27]

Making available art prints was also a way to market the product to women. These pictures, with titles like "Health and Beauty," were free to druggists, who would then offer them to their customers when the ladies purchased Tonic. Also given to Tonic customers, on request, were a series of promotional calendars. Each calendar had a different theme. In Table 3.2 below are some of the titles and the year they were available.

The druggist was a primary audience for the campaign, because the product was available only in retail drugstores. Druggists could purchase the product either from a wholesale druggist or directly from Pabst.

The trade journals for druggists had many ads about Tonic. Some of the journals that promoted the product were *Apothecary and Spatula, Bulletin of Pharmacy, Druggists Circular, Midland Druggist, Modern Druggist, Pharmaceutical Era,* and *Retail Druggist*. The themes in the ads included "increase your sales," "get more dollars," "cash in," and "supply the demand."[28] A drugstore frequently had a soda fountain, which was another revenue-making opportunity. Pabst gave pharmacists colorful printed material to promote new beverage combinations with the Tonic. One letter to a pharmacist read: "We think the public will appreciate the idea of combining a Malt Extract with Cream."[29]

Frequently, Pabst offered incentives for druggists. In one letter dated 1899, the pharmacist was offered a "mammoth triple window display figure" for the product.[30] Also, he received 100 cards

TABLE 3.2

Calendar Name	*Year*
Stork Calendar	1904
Oriental Calendar	1905
Indian Calendar	1906
American Girl	1907
Jewel Calendar	1908
Rose Girl Calendar	1909

of a colorful print that had been reduced and imprinted with the drugstore's name and address.

Druggists were encouraged to enter a contest, sponsored by Pabst, for the best window display about Tonic. Cash prizes were awarded, and the winners were written up in both the Pabst promotional material and one trade journal for the pharmacist, *Pharmaceutical Era*.[31]

Pharmacists were paid by the brewery to distribute the Secret Booklets in their neighborhoods. About 1900, Pabst sent a brochure to druggists that said: "We frequently furnish our little books for distribution from house to house, put the druggist's card on them, and pay him for having them distributed."[32]

The Tonic was referred to as a proprietary medicine by Pabst. In April 1909, a Pabst promotional letter to pharmacists stated:

> As a result, perhaps, of the recent prohibition agitation a number of retail druggists in various places throughout the United States, appear to be apprehensive as to their liability for selling malt extracts. In order that these druggists may have no hesitancy in handling Pabst Extract, The "Best" Tonic, we desire to call their attention to the letter which we reproduce on this page. This letter, sent to us on May 12, 1908, by J. G. Capers, Commissioner of Internal Revenue, rules that Pabst Extract, the 'Best' Tonic, is not classed as a beverage or a malt liquor, but comes under the heading of proprietary medicines and is so recognized by the United States Government.[33]

Pabst wanted to deter dealers from selling Tonic below the recommended price. Therefore, the brewery was willing to help druggists organize into a trade association that coincidentally agreed with the Pabst policies on price setting. One promotional brochure for druggists decreed the following: "We believe that the retail drug trade should be organized. We believe that by standing together, the retail druggists of the United States can check a great many demoralizing trade abuses that now prevail.... We are interested in the good work of organizing the drug trade, and desire to contribute to its success in a practical way."[34]

In 2 years, the Tonic sales division of Pabst was self-sufficient.[35] Also, Tonic sales supported all its own extensive promotion.

The Tonic was often sold by a middleman or wholesale druggist. In one case, a salesman for Tonic wrote to Pabst, "Your Health and Beauty picture is the greatest lever for business I have ever seen; I have sold thirteen casks of 'Best' Tonic with your offer. I am just sufficiently superstitious not to let my record stop at that."[36]

A 1902 promotional flyer from Pabst said if 2 million of anything are sold in one year, it must be a pretty good thing. That, not so coincidentally, was the number of bottles of Pabst Malt Extract sold that year.[37]

In a promotional listing of its products, Pabst included Tonic with Pabst Blue Ribbon Beer, Pabst Export, Pabst Bohemian, and Red, White and Blue.[38] To the company, Tonic was a beer product like the others. In one photograph of the Pabst products, the heading read, "The Bottled Beers of the Pabst Brewing Company"; included in the lineup of bottles is "Best" Tonic. A subheading read "for family and table use."

A letter from a customer in 1905 said: "I have used your Malt Extract with great success and must say it is my standby when I am not feeling very good (as well as the rest of your beverages)."[39] "Best" Tonic paid for a regular 5-inch ad in a Wisconsin Anti-Prohibition publication in 1888.[40] "Malt Extract" thus became a term for one of Pabst's several beer products. The 1905 editions of *Pharmacopoeia* and *Dispensatorium*, the official reference volumes for druggists, said that druggists sold a product called "Extractum Malti." However, by 1910, there is no mention of Malt Extract. It could be that the term may have been usurped by the brewery industry's tonic as malt extract.

"Malted Milk," especially as patented in 1883 by the Horlich Company in Wisconsin, was becoming an accepted part of the culture. It was the original malted milk, used in nervous disorders, as a sedative, as a vehicle for the administration of hypnotics, in the treatment of neurasthenia, and for drug addicts.[41]

The Milwaukee Pharmaceutical Association in 1900 sent a letter to druggists requesting cooperation in maintaining prices of proprietary preparations, including "Best" Tonic. The resolution was as follows: "Every druggist who has been selling 'Best' Tonic at a price less than 25 cents is expected to sell it at the regular established price in the future."[42]

Testimonies from many doctors appeared in Pabst promotional material. For example, a Dr. Bailey wrote, " I have used Pabst Malt Extract in a case of neurasthenia (nervous debility) with great benefit to the patient."[43] On January 27, 1910, Dr. Croxdale of Oklahoma wrote, "I have two very stubborn cases upon whom I desire to try your 'Extract' as I have never had the pleasure of using it but a brother physician told me a few days ago that it is the only tonic.… P. S. Would be pleased to receive one of your handsome calendars."[44] In 1889, a doctor from Brooklyn wrote, "Have noticed your 'ad' of Pabst Extract in the Medical Record. In addition let me inform you that I advise my debilitated patients to use Pabst. I therefore beg you to send me a copy of the Pabst Calendar Girl, which when I look at it, shall always remind me of the 'beer that made Milwaukee famous.'"[45]

The "Best" Tonic was judged a perfect malt extract by the medical profession. Doctors wrote articles in medical journals extolling "Best" Tonic.[46] In 1898, one nurse wrote, "It is the best Tonic I have used in my nine years as nurse. It is superior to all others for nursing mothers." Similar endorsements from nurses came from around the country, including New York, Pennsylvania, Kansas, Iowa, and Colorado.[47] In 1909, Maud Oglesby, a nurse, wrote, "I saw your ad in 'The Trained Nurse,' a calendar to every nurse. I am a nurse and use Pabst Extract with my patients. Please send at once. I find your Extract to be the very best."[48]

As mentioned earlier, most sales of "Best" Tonic were made in drugstores. One ad said: "The Best Tonic can be bought at any drug store. It is sold by seven druggists out of eight throughout the United States."[49]

Drugstores at that time were like mini-department stores and sold items like dry goods, candy, health aids, drugs, and liquor. They also typically had a soda fountain. Farrington (1914), who wrote *Making a Drug Store Sell*, noted that druggists had to treat their stores like any business that demands advertising. Chapter titles in his book include "The Soda Water Trade," "How I Pushed Cigars," "Side Lines and Schemes," "Advertising for Special Days," and "Starting Up the Candy Business."

Mason (1915) recommended using any of the many products in the drugstore for a special display in the window. The goods could include baby supplies, bath requisites, cameras, cards, cigars, cold creams, extracts, hair tonic, magazines, paints, razors, shampoo preparation, school supplies, soap, spices, toilet cream, and tonic—to name a few.

In the minutes from a board meeting held on July 5, 1919, it was noted that Drake Brothers Pharmacy in Milwaukee closed out its liquor department, thus resulting in a large cash balance for the company.[50] Perhaps this was a foreshadowing of Prohibition.

In 1904, at Dunning and Summer Druggists in Madison, Wisconsin, their daybook/journal recorded that W. M. Coffman bought liquor every other week including port, whiskey, sherry, white rose, rye whiskey, and bay rum. Some of the other items sold at that time were a hair brush, nail brush, shampoo, prescriptions, cigars, thermometer, toilet paper, caster oil, bee's wax, salad oil, toilet soap, olive oil, flax seed, and plaster.[51]

In the Pabst company publication for wholesalers of 1913, Drake Brothers was commended for their window display of "Best" Tonic. These words of advice appeared: "Don't just urge the dealer to give window space to the Extract, but offer to help him make the trim."[52]

Drake Brothers Pharmacy, started in 1859, was located in downtown Milwaukee on Michigan and Water Streets. The four-story drugstore was described in a directory of Milwaukee businesses published in 1892: "The retail store is elegantly fitted up, and is fully stocked with pure, fresh drugs and chemicals, mineral waters, proprietary medicines, toilet and fancy articles, physicians' and surgeons' requisites, and everything usually found in a first class establishment."[53]

Testimonials for "Best" Tonic came from all over the country. A printer from Kansas wrote, "I have had occasion to use your Malt Extract and find it to be one of the best tonics on the market, and absolutely up to the advertising matter of your company—The 'Best' Tonic, one that builds up and strengthens if taken regularly and consistently."[54] An executive from a varnish company in New York wrote in 1908 that his wife had recently used the Tonic after suffering what the doctors diagnosed as nervous exhaustion. In three days she was up and around the house, had an excellent appetite, slept like a child, and made a most marvelous recovery. In 1910, J. B. Crompton of Selma, Alabama, wrote, "It gives me pleasure to say that I was greatly benefited by using The Best

Tonic several years ago after recovering from a long spell of Typhoid fever, and I have recommended it frequently to my friends."[55] William Lachenmaier, who owned the School of Physical Culture, wrote in 1902 that he used 'Best' Tonic himself and also prescribed it for his patients.[56]

In the *Chicago Daily Tribune* of November 21, 1924, pharmacists declared their obligation to furnish medicine that may have intoxicating liquor in it. The Cramton Bill, supported by the Anti-Saloon League, wanted all liquor-based medicines to be regulated by Prohibition. The National Association of Retail Druggists wanted to continue to sell intoxicating liquor as medicine and had gathered in Chicago to organize against the Cramton Bill.[57]

In 1895, Baltimore druggists were to be entrapped for the sale of "Best" Tonic, which some people considered a liquor and therefore subject to the Internal Review Tax. Pabst insisted that "Best" Tonic was being sold as a medicine and therefore druggists did not need a license.[58]

In a lengthy article in *The Pharmaceutical Era* of October 30, 1902, a pharmacist named Wilbert, chastised those druggists who considered profit over helping their customers. He thought that when a proprietary product was advertised in popular journals and its manufacturer offered an incentive to the druggist, that product ought not be sold as medicine. Wilbert asserted:

> No respectable medical practitioner would willingly lend his influence to the development of [such] a compound. Campaigns that make a product well known and therefore called the best ought be put under more intense scrutiny. How a doctor can endorse a product and then receive remuneration of some sort is also a serious question. The cheap advertising rates of medical journals enables the product to become well-known to the medical community and ensures the manufacturer a hefty return on his investment.[59]

Prohibition began in 1920 and lasted until 1933. During that time, "Best" Tonic was still 2½% alcohol (Cochran, 1948).

The Pabst Brewery enjoyed *symbolic capital*. The capital was linguistic, employing an extensive promotional campaign to get the product known and thus accepted. Pharmacists and other members of the medical community came to the aid of Pabst in order to promote the Tonic.

Also, the brewery, as an organization, was part of the *habitus* of that culture. Everybody had to be careful of drinking water and milk at the turn of the century. The brewery knew that a bottled product that wasn't sold as beer would be accepted in the culture.

The *power* of the brewery enabled it to win over the Internal Revenue and the Colombian Exhibition to its position. The government agreed with Pabst that the beverage was not beer but a medicine. The Columbian Exhibition, cited earlier as an important international manufacturing and agricultural show, gave Pabst "Best" Tonic its sanction by calling it a clean and worthwhile malt and hops product.

Finally, the ability of Pabst to turn a beer into a medicine through *language* is a sign of the relationship between language and the culture. Although there were many tonics on the market, Pabst was the company with the strongest voice to call its product a food or medicinal product. In that naming, Pabst was joined by other significant groups and opinion leaders in the culture; such as pharmacists, the government, doctors, nurses, and journalists.

The issue here is not simply that Pabst sold "Best" Tonic, but that the culture affirmed it as a worthwhile product. The secondary market that Pabst was trying to reach, women, were the people who were frequently featured in the promotional material and who were more likely to go to the drugstore for such a beer product than to the local saloon.

The major research question under study in this chapter was to understand how the text, Pabst "Best" Tonic, was produced, distributed, and used from 1888 to 1956. A minor research question was how the medical community and the government aided Pabst in coding the product as a medicinal food.

Bourdieu asked how promotional language of a particular time can exert its power in the culture. The brewery was in power to promote a product as something other than what it actually was. The public accepted the definition of that product from the brewery organization. Only the Anti-Saloon League and an isolated pharmacist or two did not accept that definition: They knew and said that the product was alcohol, but their voices were clearly among the minority.

This case of public relations practice shows that the promotion of a product needs to be open to deconstruction. It is not that "Best" Tonic was not a medicine; it's that the brewery and opinion leaders said it was medicine in their public discourse. The social history surrounding the public relations of Tonic provides the evidence.

The objective of this chapter was to deconstruct public relations practice. Cultural studies was proposed as a theory and method. The review of literature found several studies of promotional material using cultural studies.

Cultural studies looks at the text produced in a particular culture and the circumstances in which it was distributed and consumed. In that process, one examines the ideology, power, and any unheard minority voice to construct a social history of the question. Bourdieu's social theory provided a cultural studies framework to view the historical data for this case.

The case study centered on the Pabst Brewing Company of Milwaukee. At the end of the nineteenth and start of the twentieth centuries, Pabst produced a product, called "Best" Tonic. With the support of the medical community as well as the government, the culture accepted this product as a medicinal food.

Public relations can be defined as planned communication to motivate publics to support a cause, service, organization, or product. As seen in this case, the public relations forms of communication can include advertising, editorial material, special events, promotional material like the Secret booklets, and even window displays.

Bourdieu asserted that power in a society belongs to the one who has symbolic capital. Symbolic capital is expressed through language. In this case, a powerful company like Pabst expressed its symbolic capital regarding Tonic through its extensive public relations discourse. Pabst produced a text called Tonic that was distributed and consumed in the culture.

There were some voices in the culture that said they would not give the meaning of medicine to a product like Tonic; but these voices were not very strong. Even through Prohibition, Pabst continued to produce Tonic with both high- and low-level alcohol content.

The next step to continue this line of research would be to see how women and the elderly were designated by Pabst as specific target publics for a beer product. Usually only men patronized saloons, which were often owned by the large breweries. Therefore, Pabst produced its "Best" Tonic to reach working women, mothers, pregnant women, women fighting "anemia" or nervousness, and men and women whose health was degenerating because of old age. The product was sold at drugstores, which were safer places for women and the elderly than were corner saloons. Thus, one might argue that age and gender were represented as part of the promotion of the product.

The general public at the turn of the century was unaware of the extensive, planned public relations discourse generated by the Pabst Brewery, the medical community, and the government in regards to "Best" Tonic. There seems to be little reason to doubt that the same thing could happen today whenever the public is offered any new product, including a new medicine.

It is important that public relations practice be open to a critical, cultural studies perspective. Deconstructing of public relations works to keep a democratic society healthy.

REFERENCES

Apple, M. (1992). Constructing the captive audience: Channel One and the political economy of text. *International Studies in Sociology of Education, 2*(7), 107–131.

Bourdieu, P. (1991). *Language and symbolic order.* Cambridge, MA: Harvard University Press.

Cochran, T. (1948). *The Pabst Brewing Company.* New York: New York University Press.

Coffin, J. G. (1994). Credit, consumption, and images of women's desires: Selling the sewing machine in late nineteenth century France. *French Historical Studies, 18*, 749–783.

Curtin, P. (1995, August). *Textual analysis in mass communication studies: Theory and methodology.* Paper presented at the annual meeting of the Association for Education in Journalism and Mass Communication, Washington, DC.

Downard, W. (1980). *Dictionary of the history of the American brewing and distilling industries.* Westport, CT: Greenwood.

Farrington, F. (1914). *Making a drug store pay.* New York: Ronald Press.

Fine, G. (1977). Popular culture and social interaction: Production, consumption, and usage. *Journal of Popular Culture, XI*(2), 453–465.
Hon, L. (1993). *Towards a feminist theory*. Presentation at the annual meeting of the Association for Education in Journalism and Mass Communication, Kansas City.
Hummon, D. (1988). Tourist worlds: Tourist advertising, ritual, and American culture. *Sociological Quarterly, 29*(2), 179–202.
Kellner, D. (1995). No respect! Disciplinarity and media studies: Media communications vs. cultural studies. *Communication Theory, 5*(2), 162–177.
Mason, H. B. (Ed.). (1915). *Window displays for druggists* (3rd Ed.). Detroit: E. G. Swift.
Miller, R. (1991). Selling Mrs. Consumer: Advertising and the creation of suburban socio-spatial relations, 1910–1930. *Antipode, 23*(3), 263–306.
Min, E. J. (1992). Can political economy of communication be incorporated with cultural studies in postmodern era? ERIC Document E0351735. 28 pp.
Mintz, L. (1983). Recent trends in the study of popular culture: Since 1971. *American Studies International, XXI*(5), 90–103.
Postman, N. (1994). *Technopoly*. New York: Vantage.
Still, B. (1948). *Milwaukee: The history of a city*. Madison: State Historical Society of Wisconsin.
Toth, E., & Heath, R. (1992). *Rhetorical and critical approaches to public relations*. Hillsdale, NJ: Lawrence Erlbaum Associates.
Wernick, A. (1991). *Promotional culture: Advertising, ideology and symbolic expression*. London: Sage.
Wilcox, D. L., Alt, P., & Agee, W. (1995). *Public relations strategies and tactics* (4th ed.). New York: HarperCollins.
Williams, R. (1974)."Communications as cultural science. *Journal of Communication, 24*(3), 17–23.
Williams, R. (1993). Advertising: The magic system. In S. During (Ed.), *The cultural studies reader* (pp. 320–336). London: Routlege.

ENDNOTES

[1]Box 4, Brewery Archives, Milwaukee, WI: Milwaukee Historical Society.
[2]Promotional book from Pabst. Scrapbook #8, p. 67. Brewery Archives, Milwaukee, WI: Milwaukee Historical Society.
[3]Ad in *Commercial America*, May 1917. Scrapbook #9, p. 76. Brewery Archives, Milwaukee, WI: Milwaukee Historical Society.
[4]Ad in *What-To-Eat*, October 1901, Book 11, N. 4. Back cover. Breweries Collection, Box 1, File 5. Milwaukee, WI: Milwaukee Historical Society.
[5]*Fiftieth Anniversary: Pabst Milwaukee*, 1894. Box 1, Pabst File. Breweries Collection, Milwaukee, WI: Milwaukee Historical Society.

[6]Ibid.

[7]Correspondence from Charles H. Fuller, dated December 2, 1911. Scrapbook #21, p. 184. Breweries Collection, Milwaukee, WI: Milwaukee Historical Society.

[8]Correspondence from Humiston, Keeling & Co., dated November 15, 1887. Scrapbook #5, p. 6. Breweries Collection, Milwaukee, WI: Milwaukee Historical Society.

[9]*Face to face: A little talk with you.* A flyer for druggists. Circa 1890's. Box 1. File #4. Pabst. Breweries Collection, Milwaukee, WI: Milwaukee Historical Society

[10]Interview with John Steiner, Pabst historian, June 17, 1995, Milwaukee, WI.

[11]Scrapbook #5, p. 57. Breweries Collection, Milwaukee, WI: Milwaukee Historical Society.

[12]Two-page flyer, letter to "Doctor," 1902. Scrapbook #20, p. 221. Breweries Collection, Milwaukee, WI: Milwaukee Historical Society.

[13]*Commercial America,* May 1917. Scrapbook #9, p. 76. Breweries Collection, Milwaukee, WI: Milwaukee Historical Society

[14]Ad in *What-To-Eat,* January 1902, Book 12, N. 1. Back cover. Breweries Collection, Box 1, File 5, Milwaukee, WI: Milwaukee Historical Society

[15]Interview with the brewmeister, August 1995. Commonwealth Brewery, Boston, MA.

[16]Article Porter (1989), *New Encyclopedia Britannica* (vol. 2, p. 45).

[17]*Wedding Secrets,* a booklet from Pabst Brewery, circa 1900. Box 1, File #4. Pabst Advertising, Breweries Collection, Milwaukee, WI: Milwaukee Historical Society.

[18]*Charm Secrets,* a booklet from Pabst Brewery, 1897. Box 1. The Award is dated in the booklet as May 17, 1894. Breweries Collection, Milwaukee, WI: Milwaukee Historical Society.

[19]An ad for Pabst Best Tonic, dated 1914. Scrapbook #1, p. 48. Breweries Collection, Milwaukee, WI: Milwaukee Historical Society.

[20]Box 2, Pabst Advertising. Breweries Collection, Milwaukee, WI: Milwaukee Historical Society.

[21]1909 Publicity Campaign for Best Tonic. Box 2, Pabst Advertising. Breweries Collection, Milwaukee, WI: Milwaukee Historical Society.

[22]1914, Tonic Advertising. Breweries Collection, Milwaukee, WI: Milwaukee Historical Society.

[23]*Fiftieth Anniversary: Pabst Milwaukee* 1894. Box 1, Pabst File. Breweries Collection, Milwaukee, WI: Milwaukee Historical Society.

[24]Scrapbook #3. Breweries Collection, Milwaukee, WI: Milwaukee Historical Society.

[25]Scrapbook #4, pp. 34, 35, 1909. Breweries Collection, Milwaukee, WI: Milwaukee Historical Society.

[26]American Institute of the History of Pharmacy. Collected Prescription Books, 1856–1910. Kopf Pharmacy Ledger, 1892–1897. MSS 726. Box 18 of 18. Madison, WI: State Historical Society of Wisconsin.

[27]Ad in *Dressmaking at Home*, October 1910, Scrapbook #19, p. 118. Breweries Collection, Milwaukee, WI: Milwaukee Historical Society

[28]1914 Tonic Advertising. Breweries Collection, Milwaukee, WI: Milwaukee Historical Society.

[29]1896, Scrapbook #20, p. 133. Breweries Collection, Milwaukee, WI: Milwaukee Historical Society.

[30]1894, Box 1, Pabst File #4. Breweries Collection, Milwaukee, WI: Milwaukee Historical Society.

[31]File C. 38, a, Manufacturing, Pabst Brewing Co. American Institute of the History of Pharmacy, Kremers Reference Files, F.B. Power Pharmaceutical Library. Madison, WI: University of Wisconsin.

[32]Scrapbook #20, p., 37. Breweries Collection, Milwaukee, WI: Milwaukee Historical Society.

[33]Promotional piece entitled: *Pabst Extract Best Tonic Is Recognized by the Government as a Medicinal Preparation and Sold by Leading Druggists without Violation of Internal Revenue Laws*. Box 3. Breweries Collection, Milwaukee, I: Milwaukee Historical Society.

[34]Scrapbook #20, p. 135. Breweries Collection, Milwaukee, WI: Milwaukee Historical Society.

[35]Interview with John Steiner, Pabst historian. June 17, 1995, Milwaukee, WI.

[36]April 26, 1899. Scrapbook #20, p. 129. Breweries Collection, Milwaukee, WI: Milwaukee Historical Society.

[37]Promotional flyer, 1902 or 1903. Scrapbook #20, p. 217. Breweries Collection, Milwaukee, WI: Milwaukee Historical Society.

[38]Pabst Advertising. Scrapbook #22, p. 234. Breweries Collection, Milwaukee, WI: Milwaukee Historical Society

[39]October 26, 1905. Box 2. Breweries Collection, Milwaukee, WI: Milwaukee Historical Society.

[40]Receipt dated November 20, 1888. Scrapbook #5, p. 20. Breweries Collection, Milwaukee, WI: Milwaukee Historical Society

[41]Horlick Corporation Papers, 1873–1974, p. 11. 1920 flyer. Parkside, WI: State Historical Society of Wisconsin.

[42]Letter dated November 24, 1900. Scrapbook #20, p. 177. Breweries Collection, Milwaukee, WI: Milwaukee Historical Society.

[43]Promotional Booklet #5, *Wedding Secrets*, p. 24. Box 1, File #4. Breweries Collection, Milwaukee, WI: Milwaukee Historical Society.

[44]Correspondence. Box 2. Breweries Collection, Milwaukee, WI: Milwaukee Historical Society.

[45]Ibid.

[46]Scrapbook #20, p. 39. Breweries Collection, Milwaukee, WI: Milwaukee Historical Society.

[47]Promotional flyer, *Based on Experience: Notes from Trained Nurses*, 1898. Scrapbook #20, p. 95. Breweries Collection, Milwaukee, WI: Milwaukee Historical Society.

[48]Correspondence. Box 2. Breweries Collection, Milwaukee, WI: Milwaukee Historical Society.

[49]Promotional Booklet #5, *Wedding Secrets*, p. 24. Box 1, File #4. Breweries Collection, Milwaukee, WI: Milwaukee Historical Society.

[50]Fitzgerald Family Manuscripts, MSS-1777, 1919. Milwaukee, WI: Milwaukee Historical Society.

[51]American Institute of the History of Pharmacy. Box 10, November 1903–November 1905. Dunning & Summer Druggists. Madison, WI. Day Book—Journal. Madison, WI: State Historical Society of Wisconsin.

[52]*Blue Ribbon News*, December 3, 1913, p. 7. Box 3. Breweries Collection, Milwaukee, WI: Milwaukee Historical Society.

[53]Article "Drake Brothers," p. 108. *Milwaukee of To-Day: The Cream City of the Lakes*. Milwaukee: Phoenix Publishing Co., 1892.

[54]Correspondence dated October 24, 1908. Box 2. Breweries Collection, Milwaukee, WI: Milwaukee Historical Society.

[55]Correspondence dated January 24, 1910. Box 2. Breweries Collection, Milwaukee, WI: Milwaukee Historical Society.

[56]January 10, 1902. Scrapbook #20, p. 203. Breweries Collection, Milwaukee, WI: Milwaukee Historical Society.

[57]File C. 19, *Merchandising Methods, Advertising; Promotions*. American Institute of the History of Pharmacy, Kremers Reference Files, F.B. Power Pharmaceutical Library. Madison, WI: University of Wisconsin.

[58]File C. 38, a, Manufacturing, Pabst Brewing Co. American Institute of the History of Pharmacy, Kremers Reference Files, F.B. Power Pharmaceutical Library. Madison, WI: University of Wisconsin.

[59]M. I. Wilbert. (1902, Oct. 30). "The Use and Abuse of Proprietary Medicines." *The Pharmaceutical Era*, pp. 153–155. A paper presented to the American Pharmaceutical Association, September 1902. File C. 39, k, Proprietary, Nostrum, and Panacea. American Institute of the History of Pharmacy, Kremers Reference Files, F.B. Power Pharmaceutical Library. Madison, WI: University of Wisconsin.

CHAPTER FOUR

Representation of Woman[1]

The number-one leisure activity in the United States is gardening. That translates into enormous revenues for companies that offer goods and services for the home gardener.

However, gardening can be viewed as more than designing a space with plants. To the student of culture and history, gardening is also a representation of a time and place simply because it is a material expression. For example, the plant called purple loosestrife was once considered a desirable ornamental perennial. Today, it is seen as an exotic invasive because it chokes out other plants along our highways, where it is now growing rampantly. The present concern for the environment has redefined this plant. To have it in your garden, as some people still do, is to snub the environment.

Heilenman (1994) said that the business of being a modern gardener has broadened from cutting the grass and growing a few tomatoes and dahlias to an entire lifestyle sometimes fraught with moral responsibility, social mobility, and political correctness. Therefore, a campaign in public relations to promote garden products uses public relations strategies that, at the same time, may represent a certain definition of horticulture, aesthetics, politics, and even economics. The objective of public relations is to win public support. Promotion of products and services is one form of public relations practice.

This chapter examines the coding of gender to promote garden products. A critical view of public relations practice provides the theoretical backdrop. A cultural studies approach serves as the critical theory and the basis for deconstruction of the public relations text.

A social practice like gardening is reified for a particular culture. Public relations practice is one way to reify it. Therefore, public relations needs to be understood as a cultural practice within a certain political and economic context.

The history of gardening provides some insight into how a culture defines its gardening in ways to foster power and ideology. For example, Hall (1996) noted that gardening is a lot like fashion and, in much the same way, may be taken as an image of society, of the self, and of the relationships between self and society.

The major question here is how gardening for women is coded in a media campaign to attract a share of the gardener dollars spent each gardening season. The minor research question is to examine how consumerism defines a cultural practice like gardening.

The significance of the problem and the justification for investigating it is that the media are becoming more dependent on public relations sources for information and news. The consumer, therefore, must develop a critical sense of public relations practice. In essence, the consumer needs to know how to deconstruct public relations. The press kit material used here as text is from the companies Garden Pals and UnionTools.

Butsch (1998) recently said there is a renewed interest in the history of how the media operates in this country. The impetus is coming from fields like American studies, media studies, and communication research. One view is of the media as the locus of an active audience that interacts with a text. The questions often center on how the audience uses the text for daily life. The text becomes a source of subjectivity as well as an expression of culture.

In this chapter, the text is a certain representation of gardening, particularly as represented in the media. Thus, there is a "way" to garden. There are plants more desirable than others. Gardening has its own theory as expressed by those who practice gardening: landscapers, plant growers, nurserypeople, garden writers, and finally public relations practitioners who promote garden products and services.

Christopher Lloyd, a famous English garden writer, now admits he would use the once-frowned-upon canna lilies in his garden (Carney & Dezell, 1998). This is a departure from traditional

English garden design, and so Lloyd's remarks on the subject were widely covered by the media.

Martin (1983) wrote that in eighteenth-century Williamsburg, Virginia, a garden represented a taming of the wilderness of America. The residents wanted a place of elegant living. Therefore, a British landscaper came over to design a cultured outdoor space of plantings. Williamsburg was intended to be a meeting place where gardens would be an important part of the town's culture. The city was to be the new nation's capital even though it was not a port city. For historians, Williamsburg has subsequently become an important site in American garden design.

Bell (1990) showed how the discussion of gardening by women in the nineteenth century was not in the landscape books of the period, but rather in their letters, garden notebooks, botanical paintings, and embroideries. From these texts we know that women were actively involved in gardening.

In a study of the role of women in gardening in rural Egypt, Shalaby (1991) demonstrated that the income and educational level of women indicated how they worked in the garden. For example, Shalaby's findings illustrated that the entire management of the kitchen garden was the wife's domain and responsibility. The garden was one way to represent gender differences.

Lazaridis (1995) conducted a study of market gardening in Greece, where women worked in greenhouses for produce that they would later sell. Lazaridis demonstrated the sexual inequality of gardening work. Although women work as hard or harder than men for a successful crop, women play a secondary role because only one person could be officially in charge of a greenhouse, and that was a man. Women worked in the garden but the men were listed in the local archives as the family breadwinners.

In Australia Alston (1995) traced how the census statistics underrepresent the work of women and their contribution to agriculture. Macklin (1993) also showed how gender divisions in rural society have allowed the efforts of men to be more visible and to be represented as more important by rural media.

There are names in the history of landscape design—like Christopher Lloyd, Gertrude Jekyll, and in this country, Frederick Olmsted—that are accepted as cultural icons. Gardening is a cultural practice whose expression has greater or lesser degrees of acceptance in a particular time. Men and women are involved in different ways, which make a statement about gender. For each period of gardening history, that involvement was often represented in the media of the day.

Gordon (1997) reported that many communication scholars agree that definitions of public relations are inherently rhetorical and that the formation of definitions are social processes that shape reality. He examined definitions of public relations in eight well-known public relations texts. His approach was a critical view of public relations, and he studied the texts for that purpose.

Martinson (1996) asserted that the public relations practitioner ought not simply accept the macro setting of the public relations campaign, and thus critique only a certain situation. Martinson opened up the question of a cultural approach to public relations criticism, based on the culture in which the campaign is produced, rather than a criticism of the promotion of a particular product or service.

Therefore, public relations as a way to present products and services to a particular society is a cultural practice that needs to be open to critical analysis. One critical approach is cultural studies. Cultural studies looks at the representations in the culture for a particular society that are the ways that people produce meanings for themselves. The representations are produced by those in power and are ways to materialize the power of one group over another.

Giroux (1994) suggested that educators (and one might add public relations practitioners) are not simply chroniclers of history and social change or recipients of culture, but instead are active participants in its construction. His is a different way to look at education. The model fits for public relations practice as well. Public relations professionals are a conduit for an ideology and power of one group over another. They are not simply a mirror or a channel for messages.

Cultural studies, according to Giroux, means that we look at culture as an activity, unfinished and incomplete. Public relations practitioners must be accountable ethically and politically for the stories they produce, the claims they make on social memories, and the images of the future they deem legitimate (Giroux, 1994).

Agger (1992) argued that cultural studies is inherently a radical activity in that it offers a method of reading and deconstructing cultural hegemony, thus enlarging the realms of freedom and imagination.

What is needed in this research is a paradigm to deconstruct public relations messages. Such a paradigm is cultural studies, a view of culture as representation of power. Public relations material is defined as a system of legitimizing power as located in a definition of age, gender, economic status, and so on.

The question at hand is the representation of gardening as produced by public relations professionals in order to market certain products and services. We want to ask questions about the meanings that such material has for the culture.

Wright (1997) noted that in our culture, the broad and often unintended messages of advertising (and public relations) and commercial speech in general are not significantly contested by any substantial coalition of cultural forces. Sayre (1993) proposed that one look at public relations material from a semiotic view, thus trying to understand the coding of a message in a particular culture. He suggested that we read material culture as symbolic of the values and ideology of the culture. Writers, photographers, and public relations professionals are all involved in producing that material culture.

Today there are many books and periodicals about gardening available on the market. There are public relations firms that specialize in promoting the green industry. Where do we first begin to look for a critical view of gardening?

A book that analyzed the media's discussion of gardening in a critical way came from Hoyles (1995). He posed the question of what gardening has to do with politics. Isn't gardening simply an escape from daily activities? We seek it for leisure. Although Hoyles discussed gardening as an English cultural activity, he pointed out how gardening was often used to form a class division, to make a statement about gender, and to establish a division of labor. He concluded that the representation of gardening constructs a division of class, gender, and taste.

The method in this chapter to investigate the representations in public relations materials is *textual analysis* as Curtin (1995) discussed it. She distinguished among content analysis, discourse analysis, and finally textual analysis. Content analysis is counting the number of times a term appears in the text, whereas discourse analysis may look at interpersonal conversation. Curtin's definition of textual analysis means understanding the text as a culturally constructed form of ideology. Therefore, we look at the text in terms of its production and consumption in a particular culture.

Curtin defined deconstructing the text as the goal of textual analysis. To question the ideas raised in the text becomes a critical step. The preferred meaning, which the authors want us to get, needs to be decoded within a certain hegemonic framework.

Hall (1975) maintained that textual analysts need to demonstrate why their interpretation is most plausible by including as much of the original text as possible. He viewed textual analysis as a method for cultural studies.

Vaillancourt (1987) noted that text-centered analysis revolves around not what the text says (its apparent content or the ideas it purports to express), but instead what it fails to say or what it suggests by innuendo. The text's contradictions, inconsistencies, and flaws are of more interest than are its context, origins, or the author's reason for writing it.

In doing a critical analysis of school textbooks, Apple (1992) asserted that the meaning of a text is not necessarily intrinsic to it. As poststructuralist theories would have it, meaning is the product of a system of differences into which the text is articulated. Thus, there is not one meaning—there are many. The meanings (often contradictory) arise in dialogue with the text. We use the text according to our gender, age, and class experience. Thus, the text is important as a way to understand self within a particular culture.

For example, in looking at a Banana Republic public relations text, Lester (1992) found that the ideology of colonialism toward Third World cultures is very much alive today and, in fact, is used to sell products. Lester's work was based on a textual analysis of Banana Republic's mail-order catalogues.

The feminist interpretation of gardening books was Harris' (1994) focus. She looked at books by women about gardening from 1870 to 1920. Although the garden writer often admitted ignorance, it was a gesture of the writer to express powerlessness as a stepping stone to self-identity for the female reader because, in a male-dominated environment, she was not supposed to know anything about gardening and certainly not to write about the subject. Harris' was one critical look at gardening texts to understand the role of women in the culture.

Stern (1996) analyzed advertising through textual analysis. She proposed a threefold strategy: identification of the signs and symbols in the ad; construction of its meaning; and finally, deconstruction, or to make hidden assumptions over and to give voice to silent, cultural influences. Stern said that hers is a postmodernist approach to language that is what is currently needed in communication research, as opposed to the more common modernist approach of looking at the text in which meaning is "closed" and in finite denotations. She complained that most promotional research is done in a modernist approach.

Although Stern's work is primarily in advertising, she lent a conceptual framework to textual analysis for public relations critical theory building. She relied on the advertising text (in this case, dogfood coupons) as the way to understand ideology and power in the culture. The text is the locus of multiple meanings that clash. Stern's analysis of the dogfood described the human/animal world in which the human needs to keep the animal in control. The animal becomes identified as a family friend. Other cultures see animals as part of nature and therefore as often uncontrollable. As we know, some cultures even eat the animals we call "pets." She concluded that the dogfood ad was selling an ideology as well as dogfood.

Stern recommended that more research in planned communication like public relations use the textual analysis approach based on postmodernist literary theory, in which what the text does not say is as important as what it does say. The text is a canvas of differences proposed by those in power, who often admit that their work in word and image seeks to have the consumer identify with the product. Stern advocated deconstructing the promotional text.

As mentioned earlier, this chapter relies on the public relations material from two companies—Garden Pals and UnionTools—that sell gardening products. Their press kits were made available to the author.

The problem to be studied is as follows: How does one differentiate woman as gardener? How does one promote a gender-specific gardening tool?

Stern's threefold strategy for textual analysis is followed in this discussion of the public relations text. Although she used the method to discuss advertising, it is also possible to apply the method to a discussion of public relations material. First, we identify the symbol through a discussion of the words and imagery included in the text. Second, we construct its meaning by looking at the meaning created by the choice and placement of imagery and words. The cultural relevance of a certain form of coding, or its intended meaning, is important. Third, we deconstruct the text by pointing out the ideology within the words and symbols used. What is left out of the words that are used? What are the implications of the choice of words?

First, we look at Garden Pals, and then we examine UnionTools. A summary discussion follows each case. Finally, a commentary concludes the cultural implication with a discussion on the larger issues of gardening, gender, and culture.

Case 1: Garden Pals

A press release from Garden Pals introduces the product in a heading that reads: "Garden Gals Introduces Garden Gals Garden Tools Specifically Designed by Women for Women."

Women are responsible for producing these new garden tools. The release continues with a double quote: "Tools created 'to fit' a woman's gardening needs." The words "to fit" appear to stand out and emphasize that the product will fit the woman gardener.

"Garden Gals products, which carry a lifetime warranty, are created by women for women, from the smaller-scaled, lightweight design to the contemporary fashion colors." This sentence appears in lines 8 to 10 of the release. It is worth noting that the sentence includes the expression "by women for women."

The garden tools are then described as "perfect for small hands and gardeners with lessened hand strength." The power of the product is described in these terms: "The scaled-down design for smaller hands has full cutting potential but will not crush or damage even the most delicate stems."

What follows next is a discussion of three of the tools. The multipurpose scissors will cut through anything "while saving fingernails." Then the Houseplant/Bonsai pruner is described as exceptionally lightweight with molded handles, made of a "Tender Touch" material.

The language used in these phrases from the press release emphasize ease of use, benefits for the more delicate gardener, lightweight material, protection of the gardener's fingernails, and most important, that the tools are made by women for women. The tools will fit the woman as clothing fits her. They easily become as close to her as her clothes.

The focus of the language is therefore that women gardeners now have their own tools for gardening. Although the female gender is the more delicate gender, women can still do the tough job of gardening.

The words of the release raise many questions for the critical viewer. The focus on women as weak and more delicate is here, but why? According to the National Gardening Association, women do as much gardening as men. Doesn't that show their strength and ability?

These tools are made by women for women. That means women ought to jump on board, because members of their own gender were involved in designing these tools. But what if they were designed by men? Would that mean the tools are not suitable for a woman?

Case 2: UnionTools

The release from UnionTools says "Lady Gardener tools evolved from research showing a need for strong, forged garden tools for women that are smaller, have slimmer handles, are lighter in weight and attractive beyond what is found in traditional lawn and garden products." The tools are described as strong but light. Their designs were predicated from research on what women wanted in the garden.

The result of that research is described in double quotes as a "perfect fit" for women. The tools are painted in colors of black, deep burgundy, and a brasslike color. The tools from the UnionTools Company were also designed by women for women. This gives them added value, because men were not involved in their creation.

The description of the tools in the release position them as being easy for a woman to use because they are light, but still powerful enough to do the job. The colors of the tools are highlighted because colors are important to women. They fit women like clothing fits a woman. The tools are therefore described as a perfect fit for a woman.

The emphasis of the release is on color and the lightweight quality of the tools. Because of these features, the tool is perfect for a woman whose judgment is based on color and the low weight of tools. Positioning women as people who judge by color and how much things weigh might imply that a woman's values are superficial. She ought not be taken too seriously, even in the case of gardening.

On one level, garden tools are certainly an unnecessary product, because their purpose is simply to facilitate work in the garden. Yet, even here, women must be identified by their need to judge things based on color and weight.

The fact that women gardeners are responsible for the tools is an attempt in the text to validate them. Some women say that women gardeners need special tools for their special feminine way of gardening, so we produce them for all women.

The two companies both construct a definition of gardening as female. For what reason? Their effort to discuss garden tools as "female" may be a way of helping women take back gardening as their own. Men cannot have all the power in this area. Power must also belong to women who are soft and delicate, and therefore more suitable for gardening.

Framing the gardening tools as delicate, colorful, but strong is a way of saying they are female but still can do the work. This may seem the sentiment in the workforce today: Women are delicate but can still do the work of a man.

The fact that the tools are designed by women is a form of endorsement for the tools. If women designed them, then they must be good. But do all women share this image of women? The language of the press releases is gender specific: Women are coded as soft, fragile, and emotional.

As stated at the beginning of this chapter, gardening is the number-one leisure activity in the country. According to the National Gardening Association (National Gardening Survey, 1993–1994), 51% of gardeners in the United States are men and 49% are women. Women participate equally in all the activities of the garden in which men engage, with only a slightly lower number of women fertilizing, edging, and mowing the lawn. On a regular basis both men and women are found in the garden, doing the same kinds of work.

Yet, according to the public relations material of the two tool companies, women need to feel "feminine" in the garden. Therefore, the companies have produced tools especially for her. The tools, however, are coded in language that does not coincide with the cultural reality of gardening. Perhaps it is because an annual expenditure of over $22 million dollars on garden retail makes the area a lucrative marketing zone.

The production of garden tools for women is simply a way for these two companies to get a part of all those dollars spent on gardening. The coding of tools, therefore, is market driven. A consumer-driven image may guide both the production and promotion of gardening products and services.

The companies' public relations material constructs gender differences for the sake of promoting gardening sales. However, the public relations material is not selling just a product, but also a construction of gender. Do we want to see gender coded in this way? Why should women stand out in the garden?

We do not just garden. We garden as social actors according to the ideology and value system of our culture. At this point, gardening, like so much of modern culture, is driven by the theory that those in power (corporations) tell us how to think about and practice social activities like gardening.

There has to be a critical voice speaking out about how a practice like gardening is constructed, because the "other" voice—rather than the corporate one—needs to be heard and recognized. A critical theory must be used to view the public relations text for gardening products and services. If a leisure activity like gardening is coded to produce gender differences, what can be said about the more "serious" areas of life, like medicine, government, education, and entertainment?

Gardening, because it is a leisure activity, could be a gauge to see how the voice of difference is constructed in the culture. The promotion of gardening is sometimes a promotion of gender differences as well.

The public relations person's task is to promote a product or service. In that process, he/she uses words from the culture that will do the job. Must the writer who needs to sell female garden tools to women use female descriptors like *soft, delicate, gal, colorful,* and *great fit?*

For some women gardeners, these words will do the job. Others will not respond at all. Yet another segment will be outraged at these messages.

This chapter has sought to demonstrate that the mundane job of promoting gardening tools is also a way of constructing gender differences. The public relations writer cannot simply say, "I'm just doing my job. Someone has to promote these products."

Public relations is an important social practice that needs to be open to deconstruction. Cultural studies—a way of pointing out the levels of power constructed through language—is one critical theory that is useful for such an analysis.

This chapter was limited to two garden products. Both use almost identical language to discuss the benefits of the product, which may demonstrate that the writer has a limited number of ways to construct gender for the culture. Promotion of products has a goal of increased sales, not social change or self-reflection, so the easiest and quickest way to be understood is to employ generally unquestioned codes. That is specifically what needs to be questioned: the natural or everyday way to look at things. Although the pubic relations writer may not perform that task, the public relations critic needs to address it. That has been the purpose of this chapter.

Although gardening may not be of interest to some people, it still is an important cultural practice. In the popular mind, gender differences about gardening abound: Men grow vegetables and women grow flowers; men cut the grass and women do the weeding. Where do these ideas come from? They are talked about, written about, and promoted in the media. Yet that language, and ultimately the display of power embodied in a public relations text, needs to be open to deconstruction.

REFERENCES

Agger, B. (1992). *Cultural studies as critical theory.* London: Falmer.

Alston, M. (1995). Women and their work on Australian Farms. *Rural Sociology, 60*(3), 521–552.

Apple, M. (1992). The text and cultural politics. *Educational Researcher, 21*(7), 4–11.

Bell, S. G. (1990). Women create gardens in male landscapes: A revisionist approach to eighteenth-century English garden history. *Feminist Studies, 16*(3), 471–493.

Butsch, R. (1998, April). *A new interest in history in communication research*. Presentation at the annual Meeting of the Eastern Communication Association, Saratoga Springs, NY.

Carney, B., & Dezell, M. (1998, May 13). Names and Faces. "She can't cotton to cannas." *Boston Globe*, p C2.

Curtin, P. A. (1995, August). *Textual analysis in mass communication studies: Theory and methodology*. Paper presented at the annual meeting of the Association for Education in Journalism and Mass Communication, Washington, DC.

Giroux, H. A. (1994). Doing cultural studies: Youth and the challenge of pedagogy. *Harvard Educational Review, 64*(3), 278–308.

Gordon, J. C. (1997). Interpreting definitions of public relations: Self-assessment and a symbolic interactionism-based alternative. *Public Relations Review, 23*(1), 57–66.

Hall, D. (1996). A garden of one's own: The ritual consolations of the backyard garden. *Journal of American Culture, 19*(3), 9–13.

Hall, S. (1975). Introduction. In A. C. H. Smith (Ed.), *Paper voices: The popular press and social change, 1935–1965* (pp. 11–24). London: Chatto & Windus.

Harris, D. (1994). Cultivating power: The language of feminism in women's gardening literature, 1870–1920. *Landscape Journal, 13*(2), 113–123.

Heilenman, D. (1994). *Gardening in the lower Midwest: A practical guide for the new zones 5 and* 6. Bloomington: Indiana University Press.

Hoyles, M. (1995). *Bread and roses: Gardening books from 1560 to 1960* (vol. 2). London: Pluto.

Lazaridis, G. (1995). Market gardening and women's work in Platanos, Greece. *The European Journal of Women's Studies, 2*, 441–467.

Lester, E. (1992). Buying the exotic "other": Reading the "Banana Republic" mail order catalogue. *Journal of Communication Inquiry, 16*(2), 74–85.

Macklin, M. (1993). Local media and gender relationships in a rural community. *Rural Society, 3*, 2–7.

Martin, P. (1983). Williamsburg: The role of the garden in "Making a Town." In H. C. Payne (Ed.), *Studies in eighteenth-century culture* (vol. 12, pp. 187–204). Madison: University of Wisconsin Press.

Martinson, D. L. (1996). Stimulating the moral imagination. *Public Relations Quarterly, 41*(4), 9–11.

National Gardening Association. (1994). *National gardening survey, 1993–1994*. Burlington, VT: Author.

Sayre, S. (1993). Symbolic communication: Reading material culture. *Journalism Educator, 47*(4), 13–19.

Shalaby, M. T. (1991). The role of women in Egyptian rural development. *Habitat International, 15*(4), 85–104.

Stern, B. B. (1996). Textual analysis in advertising research: Construction and deconstruction of meaning. *Journal of Advertising, 25*(3), 61–73.

Vaillancourt, P. M. (1987). Discourse analysis, post-structuralism, post-modernism, deconstruction, semiotics: A new paradigm for the social sciences? *The Polish Sociological Bulletin, 4*, 89–100.

Wright, R. G. (1997). *Selling words: Free speech in a commercial culture*. New York: New York University Press.

ENDNOTE

[1]This chapter originally appeared as "Public Relations Practice and Critical Theory: Preparation of the Gardener as Woman" in *Mass Communication Mixing Views*, edited by Jabbar A. Al-Obaidi, published in 2001. Reprinted with permission.

CHAPTER FIVE

Selling the Internet[1]

A 1996 Compaq ad said: "Over the years, a lot of people have talked about the coming of the information superhighway. The fact of the matter is, it's not coming. It's here. It's called the Internet." It appears that we will not be on the superhighway without the Net!

The federal government wanted to place the Internet in all schools. In his 1996 State of the Nation address, President Clinton promised that he would hook up every school in the country. He and Vice President Gore made newspaper headlines in their endorsement of NetDay ("Clinton, Gore," 1997).

NetDay was a day in which volunteers—either people from computer industries or parents—wire local schools for Internet access. Funding came from corporations such as Apple, Netscape, Sun Microsystems, US Robotics, Netcom, Cisco Systems, or Spyglass; or from local businesses, charities, or parent–teacher associations (PTAs).

This chapter looks at the group that sponsored NetDay in Massachusetts, held in October 1996 and April 1997. The sponsor, Mass Networks, was a computer industry partnership with public education. In this discussion, we argue that Mass Networks is a public relations activity from the computer industry.

It is not uncommon for corporations to sponsor community/business links to promote good will with the community and also provide an environment in which the product of the company has greater acceptability. For example, the Bankers Association conducts workshops in schools on check writing and budgeting, with the goal of building future customers. This is simply considered good public relations practice.

This chapter takes a critical look at one form of public relations practice from the high-tech industry, the promotion of the Internet to schools through NetDay. The critical theory to examine the campaign is cultural studies, defined as a way to study culture in order to understand the sources of power and influence represented, especially through images in the media. The goal is to deconstruct public relations practice.

There has been some criticism of hooking up schools to the Internet. One newspaper critic (McCarthy, 1996) wrote that schools with dedicated teachers would help children more than would schools dedicated to computers.

The Luddite-style response to new technology is familiar in the study of culture. Although we may not literally smash new technology, there must be some need for a critical voice protesting the latest technology. For example, in the growth of the newspaper industry in the nineteenth century, people were warned of the decay in morals that a daily press would spread to the masses. A similar outcry came with the advent of movies, radio, TV, and cable. What we learn from history is the need to listen to that voice. This chapter provides a voice critical of the latest in computer technology by questioning the values in the text of one public relations campaign to promote technology in the schools.

The research problem here is to explore the ideology of a corporate-sponsored, nonprofit organization. How does the high-tech industry encode its ideas and values within the culture? As we discuss, one way is through the promotion of NetDay.

Snyder (1996) noted that studies of technology transfer should examine all the stakeholders: governments and militaries; research institutions; manufacturers and owners of the rights to the technology and replacement parts; software developers and promoters; transfer agents, communication media, organizations, and interorganizational linkages; and individual, public, and business users. This chapter examines the technology promoters. Wilcox, Ault, and Agee (1995) pointed out that product promotion is an important form of public relations support for marketing.

The major research question here is: What is the relationship between public relations strategy and the production of values in the culture? As a planned communication form, a public relations text can be a press release, a public service announcement, a brochure, or a business/community partnership. Such a strategy is not just a way to get information out to any audience, but also a way to code values and an ideology for the culture.

Cultural studies writers who come mainly from the fields of literature and history would argue that those in power control the cultural symbols and thereby the dreams of a culture. Through such symbols, we understand ourselves and our place in the world. We used to learn who we are and where we are going through the stories of the community told and retold around a campfire. Now such communal learning comes from the images of the media. Media advertisers like Disney and McDonald's not only sell entertainment and food, they also sell quick versions of fun and satisfaction. They tell us that to be an American is to enjoy fast food and the packaged entertainment of a place like Disney World.

The minor research question here is to explore how the media often set the news agenda using public relations sources. Davis Salisbury ("Talk from the Top," 1997) maintained that the central doctrine of public relations is molding news and public opinion to match a marketing strategy. Any kind of public relations activity is a way of selling the company's product.

Unfortunately, the person reading the story in the paper often does not know that the source of the story is a press release that embodies the value system of the company. A press release is the most ordinary of public relations tools. For example, today all TV news facilities use video news releases that are packaged stories produced by the public relations staff of a company like a pharmaceutical firm extolling the benefits of a new drug. The viewer then thinks that the piece on TV's nightly news came from the local news team. It is important for consumers to understand the ways in which corporate America inserts itself in news and entertainment, so that these consumers can make an informed decision on the value of the product or service.

This chapter illustrates how public relations activity becomes both local and national news, extolling the value of a company's product. This is a significant problem to explore, because the public does not know that much in the daily press is generated by public relations. For example, there is growing controversy about the role of computer technology, like the Internet, in the schools. Gelernter (1996) wrote, "Virtually everything the Internet is selling, our children already have too much of and are choking on. The Web is a wonderful source of raw data. But our children are barely able to handle the data they already have—the databases and computer CDs and videotapes at many public libraries, the newspapers they don't read, the 24-hour news channels and c-spans they don't watch, the old-fashioned books they ignore" (p. B7).

Ehrenreich (1995) asserted that journalism is fast becoming a branch of public relations. She noted that newspaper writers are joining public relations firms as newspaper jobs dwindle. With that expertise comes an ease at getting placement in the press. Meanwhile, the reader may not know that the story has been generated by a public relations staff to get favorable coverage for its client.

The high-tech industry, although interested in getting favorable coverage, also wants to create a climate in which there will be more acceptance of its products.

This is demonstrated in this case study of Mass Networks, the community/business partnership, in which we examine its promotional materials, which include a fact sheet, sources of funding media coverage, and an organizational history. All of this material is available on the Internet.

Public relations has traditionally used product-sponsored nonprofit organizations as a way to make its product or service more attractive in the public arena. This is an accepted practice in the public relations industry.

For example, the Dairy Association may run a campaign for milk that includes images of celebrities with milk on their upper lip. This campaign has appeared in many consumer magazines. The objective is to promote a positive image of milk.

The liquor industry has traditionally used public relations to make its product more acceptable. There is some controversy over whether it is appropriate for this industry to use advertising, whereas some elements in the industry want to start targeting TV, radio, and print audiences with ads ("End of Voluntary Ban," 1997).

One public relations campaign, the Citizens for a Sound Economy, promised to spread its message that excessive EPA regulations kill businesses and stifle economic growth. This pro-Big Business group had a $5 million budget for its campaign ("Business Group," 1997).

Leading companies often turn to their trade associations for lobbying ("Leading Companies," 1994). One example is the troubled Tobacco Institute, the public relations vehicle for the tobacco industry.

There is another kind of group used as a public relations strategy, called the "consumer-related group" or the "people's group." Although it may appear to be a blend of a public interest group and a trade association, as a corporate-sponsored group its allegiance is to the corporation. In creating a public relations plan for a client, it is not unusual to recommend such a group to be the spokesperson for the corporation. Because it is such a common practice, we can assume that it works quite effectively. The terms "Citizens for," "Concerned Citizens," "Partnership," and "People for" are often in the title of the group. The consumer may be unaware that this group was generated as part of the public relations strategy of the company, industry, or trade association.

The history of the relationship between technology and culture as one of both cultural change and domination is well documented. A communication technology is never simply a tool; instead, it is always a form of supporting one way to do something over another. The path that a technology takes is usually driven by commercial interests, and subsequently the culture accepts a new form of praxis. A few examples may help illustrate this.

In 1874, the format for the typewriter was set by Remington. Other typewriters adapted it as well, including Underwood, Remington's chief rival. That is the keyboard we use today.

Radio was proposed in the early 1920s as being free of any connection with the marketplace. Yet, within a short time, pitching products over the air made radio a hit.

In the 1940s, TV became analog because the technology had to be available to as many homes as possible, and that just happened to be the form the networks were producing. Today, we are being forced to convert to digital, and the U.S. TV industry is in the shakes. The presence of cable was going to ensure more public access and community involvement. Although that has happened to some degree, cable now provides more commercial channels than we can possibly watch.

The Internet has been hailed as the greatest technology of modern time. Yet, critics argue that the Net is fast becoming a virtual peddler (Doheny-Farina, 1996).

What we see is that a communication technology changes culture in ways that support those parties who have most to gain financially from that technology. The rest of us simply accept the technology as a new "way" to communicate faster and more efficiently.

Over the generations, there have been several important social critics of the role of technology in the development of culture. They all take what we might call a cultural studies approach insofar as they point out what voices are not being heard when a new technology comes on board, and offer a critical voice as we inaugurate, in this case, the wide-scale use of the Internet in the schools.

Mueller (1970) noted that his experience has been that a deeper understanding of a technological society gives better reasons for fear of life in it. He wondered about the purposes of the few who controlled the communication technology of the country.

Innis (1972) pointed out that new communication technologies like the printing press and electronic media developed monopolies of knowledge and even nationalism. Those who control the technology have a way to control the flow of ideas.

Ong (1982) saw the lessening of the oral tradition with the insertion of electronic media, especially one-way communication forms.

Postman (1993) argued that the world has never before been confronted with information glut and has hardly had time to reflect on its consequences. Cable can give us over 150 channels, and the Net now gives us almost infinite bits of information. For what? Postman asserted that the culture surrenders to technology and we therefore live in a state of *technopoly*, in which culture is shaped by technology.

Such critics challenge us to look at what the history of new technology forms in communication have done to the culture. They ask us to place these technology forms within the context of our larger human needs and social values.

An examination of public relations practice has traditionally relied on a social science model of communication research. Thus, the goal is to see how one can make a campaign more effective. However, public relations research needs more studies that take a critical theory approach, which would be concerned with the imposition of values and ideology through the representation of one voice. That is the role of cultural studies in the history of the study of literature as well as media. Andersen (1995) maintained that journalism is being replaced by media marketing techniques that target the American public with messages intended to persuade, not to inform. The same marketing machine behind product advertising now drives much of reporting.

If public relations depends on the media to get its message out, we must open the practices of that process up to question. The role of critical theory applied to public relations practice is to deconstruct public relations.

Goldman (1992) wrote that ads reframe and position our meaningful relations and discourses to accommodate the meaning of their corporate interests. He viewed ads as not simply ads, but instead as ways to frame a meaning for us. One could apply his thought to promotional material like any public relations text and examine it in terms of how it defines self and one's place in society.

Baker (1996) called for an attribution for any promotional material that appears in the press, just as an Associated Press (AP) story is tagged. He dismissed press releases as pure advertising, simply because their purpose is to promote a product or service. He argued that an advertiser should be barred from intentional use of its economic resources to influence nonadvertising content unless the advertiser is identified to the public in a manner that suggests its influence.

Fisher and Fisher (1996) traced the history of television, which is filled with intrigue on the part of the owners of the technology. In 1939 RCA conducted the first broadcast in the United States and wanted the Federal Communication Commission to decide in its favor on the kind of TV receiver to be built and sold in this country. Fisher and Fisher asserted that, more recently, the alliance set by the government in May 1993 to recommend how to deal with digital TV in the United States was just a group of entrepreneurs trying to peddle their own system.

David Sarnoff was one of the giants of the telecommunications industry. He founded NBC in 1926 and served as both president and chairman of RCA.

Sarnoff's words at the first TV broadcast in 1939 might well be directed today to the importance of the Internet: "It is with a feeling of humbleness that I come to this moment of announcing the birth in this country of a new art so important in its implications that it is bound to affect all society. It is an art which shines like a torch of hope in a troubled world. It is a creative force which we must learn to utilize for the benefit of all mankind" (Fisher & Fisher, p. 278).

The implications of a new technology for the culture are not understood simply because it is a *new* technology, and yet it is often called a beacon of hope. The same could be said of the Internet today. Although the system has been around for a couple of decades, it is still new to many people in this country.

The role of the Net is uncertain for Doheny-Farina (1996). He noted:

> Unfortunately, communities across the nation are being undermined and destroyed by a variety of forces. Global computer networks like the Internet represent a step in the continual virtualization of human relations. The hope that the incredible powers of global computer networks can create new virtual communities, more useful and healthier than the old geographic ones, is thus misplaced. The Net seduces us and further removes us from our localities—unless we take charge of it with specific, community-based, local agendas. (p. 37)

In his critical look at the Net, Doheny-Farina wanted to make sure that students have real-time interactions with teachers and peers, and not merely access to displays of information. He wanted the Internet to connect the student to his/her local community in order to enable more local involvement. He asked his readers to bring doubt to every claim about the Net, but be committed to moving forward with it.

Cultural studies requires us to identify the operation of specific practices in a culture, how they continuously reinscribe the line between legitimate and popular culture, and what they accomplish in specific contexts. At the same time, Nelson, Treichler, and Grossberg (1992) suggested that cultural studies must constantly interrogate its own connection to contemporary relations of power. In terms of the promotion to wire schools for Internet access, one could say that we need to see how that idea becomes important to the culture: what legitimates it, and what gives that idea its power over other ideas that may or may not conflict with it.

If people think a certain way in the culture, it is because the cultural symbols *represent* the idea to them. Who are the sources behind that representation? These are the important questions derived from cultural studies as a critical theory applied to this public relations case. The promotion of Internet technology in the schools is a way to promote being, thinking, and acting. It is not simply a public relations campaign.

The major question here is: How did one corporate-sponsored public relations group called Mass Networks propose an idea that it saw as valuable for the society, but not open dialogue and argument about that idea in the community? A minor question is: How did the corporate takeover of the wiring of schools in Massachusetts come about?

To research these questions, our major resource was archival material. Webb, Campbell, Schwartz, and Sechrest (1972) asserted that archival records offer a large mass of pertinent data for many substantive areas of social science research. They are cheap to obtain, easy to sample, and the population restrictions associated with them are often knowable and controllable through data transformation and the construction of indices. Mass Networks provided much of the material itself. Therefore, we use primarily this material plus press coverage of NetDay.

Public relations critical research along the lines of a cultural studies approach relies on an examination of the promotional text. Hirston-Shea and Benoit (1996) examined a brochure produced by the Tobacco Institute as a response to the ridicule that the tobacco industry received in several "Doonesbury" cartoons. It was not just a brochure, but a rhetorical act to influence stakeholders.

This chapter looks at the larger question of how promotion of the Internet fits into the Massachusetts school system. This is the need to give an economic and political context to a text. Bird (1997) argued that it is common for cultural studies researchers to use only the text and theoretical readings to examine it. The focus here is the text—the promotional material from Mass Networks—but in the light of the cultural environment.

This method is an historical/critical approach. We examine the origin of the organization, its promotional material, and the press coverage of its major media event, NetDay. The major resources we used were archival material, interviews, secondary material, and media clippings. After our discussion, we offer a critique of that material.

Webb et al. (1972) noted that there are two major sources of bias in archival records: selective deposit and selective survival. The material we used is readily available, and we could easily look at all of it to make an argument.

Cultural studies research often uses a method called *textual analysis*. This method suggests examining the words and images of the text (e.g., the campaign material) in the light of the culture in which it is produced. The meaning of the words and pictures are therefore discerned in relation to the economic and political environment in which they are represented.

The discussion follows in this order: origin of the group called Mass Networks, funding for the group, NetDay, and media coverage of the day. Finally, we analyze the material.

The public relations printed material from the Mass Networks Education Partnership (1997a) says it is a volunteer, nonpartisan organization of people from business, government, and education, working together to bring the Internet into Massachusetts' schools. Mass Networks began in 1996. Table 5.1 lists the sources of funding for the group as follows:

The Board of Directors has 30 members: 80% are high-tech executives and 20% are educators.

TABLE 5.1
Funding Sources

Quantum	$100,000
Sun Microsystems	50,000
NYNEX	25,000
AT&T	25,000
DEC	25,000
BankBoston	22,500
Massachusetts Technology Collaborative	10,000
IDX	7,500
Wang	5,000

The mission of Mass Networks is to build the electronic infrastructure for the education system that will give teachers the tools and students the skills needed for success in the twenty-first century.

The business leaders working with Mass Networks give some combination of the following four reasons for participation:

1. They believe that it is the right thing to do, a way to give back to their community.
2. Their employees have made it clear that they want the firm to be involved.
3. They know that their firms will eventually benefit from the improvement of the education system and the increased availability of a properly trained labor force.
4. They believe that the education market will soon be an important part of their business and they want to come in on the ground floor as helpful partners.

Mass Networks sponsored two NetDays, which were held on October 26, 1996, and April 5, 1997. On both days, volunteers from the computer industry helped to wire public schools throughout the state. A similar type of program has also been held in other states around the country.

There are 2,536 public schools in the state of Massachusetts. Mass Networks reported (1997b) that about 700 or 27% were wired for the Internet.

The public relations material produces a meaning about technology in the culture. Textual analysis is a method to look at the words and images of the campaign in the light of the culture in which they are produced. There are several key points in the material that need to be discussed:

1. Business is leading the way. Mass Networks is a group started and promoted by the corporate sector.
2. The technology of the superhighway is a focus and vision that the state and our schools need to buy into if they are to stay competitive.
3. The nation's future will be better because of the growth of the computer technology industry, which will provide job opportunities and a stronger economy.

4. Education is following the lead of the business community. Education can learn what to do from business.
5. A collaborative union or partnership between the business community and the education community is a benefit to both.

The words of the campaign material need to be open to debate and dialogue because the ideology they present is the corporate voice, not necessarily the only valid voice about the future of education. Business leads the way to greater profits, but not necessarily to the benefit of the social order.

Accepting the importance of high technology, especially the Internet, means buying into a technology that is not neutral or just another way to communicate, but instead is an investment in the importance of technology as both an industry and a way of thinking about self, work, and the social order.

The campaign material proposes that the future will be improved by bringing the Internet into the classroom. It says that we will prepare our students to assume their role in the twenty-first century through the introduction of Internet technology. Education is dependent on the use of technology, especially the Internet. The collaboration is good for both entities—corporate technology and education. What educators give to the high-tech professionals for their expertise are dollars in order to purchase goods and services from them.

To illustrate the need to regard the Internet in terms of how new technology has taken a commercial route rather than becoming a source of community building, we need only look at the history of the TV and cable industries. In Table 5.2 is the new technology index, in which three industries are profiled: TV, cable, and the Internet. TV and cable have been following a similar path in becoming part of popular culture. The Internet seems to be taking the same journey.

The early proponents of all three, as Sarnoff predicted for TV, describe a vision of greater community and a smaller globe simply because of the new technology. Yet, we know that in the cases of TV and cable such a vision was put on the back burner so that commercial interests could support the growth of the technology.

TABLE 5.2
New Technology Index

	TV (1931)	*Cable (1971)*	*Internet (1997)*
Grand vision	Common good	Common good	Common good
Ownership	RCA, networks	Cable industry	Public and private
Role of government	Government-supported industry; FCC	Government-supported industry; FCC	No government control
Provider	TV networks by selling advertising time	Cable company or phone company; mainly financed by advertising and subscription	Private companies; some government sources, but somebody always pays; limited freenet
Customer	Viewer	Cable subscriber; viewer can purchase dish	Subscriber
Benefit to schools	None, because TV (except for public TV) is market driven	Very little, because it is 95% commercial, except for a few educational/special interest channels; limited distance learning	Commercial use dominates; fast becoming Virtual Peddler. Future in question???

The ownership of TV and the cable industry is private, whereas the Internet is both private and public. Internet access requires a provider, which in the majority of cases is a private company. Someone always has to pay for providing that service. TV and cable went the route of selling commercial time to support the technology. It appears that the Internet is on the same path.

Thus far, the government has taken little part in guiding the direction of the Internet, whereas the FCC obligated TV and cable to a minimum public responsibility. For example, the number of commercials on children's Saturday morning TV was limited because otherwise the broadcast industry would show a constant flow of commercials for products like cereals and toys.

The final question in the index concerns the technology's benefit to the schools. TV and cable offer little direct benefit, because they are mainly entertainment. However, there are exceptions, like some public TV programming, learning channels on cable, and limited distance learning using cable.

The benefit of the Internet to the schools is still in question, because the industry is evolving. However, the signs of that evolution are moving along commercial lines, which makes one doubt that the Internet will be much different from both TV and cable in benefitting education.

Several reasons make it necessary to deconstruct this public relations campaign. First, we live in a culture that is market driven. The hot communication technology now appears to be the Internet. One valuable market for the Internet is the education community, but it is the corporate initiative that is driving the Internet insertion into U.S. schools, as one Georgia paper claimed when reporting on a NetDay in Georgia (Loupe, 1996). Remember that one goal of Mass Networks is to sell products to the schools.

Second, educators seem to be playing a minor role in this partnership. The majority of the Mass Networks board are high-tech executives. There are many teachers who are not even sure about computers, much less the Internet. How will this technology actually play in the schools?

Third, the one voice seems to be that technology will launch our schools into the twenty-first century. The discourse is that of a non-profit group whose funding comes from the computer industry.

Fourth, the new technology index in Table 5.1 shows the history of the two other communication technologies. The ones who profit from such technologies are the business ventures. Each of the technologies promised a vision of community and a more informed society. With both TV and cable, we have become a society of consumers, not necessarily a society of more learned and caring individuals.

The campaign from Mass Networks was promoted in a culture that needs to hear other voices about technology and education. We do not need to simply accept the messages of the campaign, especially because of our history with other important communication technologies. TV and cable made promises that were not fulfilled because the marketplace drove them in a different direction. One can also see that potential in the Internet.

Every day more businesses are going on the Internet. One computer executive (Conrades, 1997) said, "Business use of the Internet is on fire. The World Wide Web is expanding at an incredible rate—even faster than the PC did a decade ago. In fact, the Net is now the fastest growing technology in economic history, attracting financial and intellectual capital at an unrelenting pace. The number of Internet hosts is growing at triple-digit rates in countries across Europe, Asia, and Latin America."

As the corporate sector assumes leadership on the Internet, the education community must come to terms with its relationship to the Internet. Who will lead? Who will follow? Whose benefit will result from the process? Who will speak for the education community? These are important questions to ask as we confront public relations strategies, like NetDay, that originate in a partnership with the computer industry.

The research goal of this chapter was to deconstruct the public relations discourse of a corporate-sponsored partnership with education. The objective was to examine how ideas about technology are spread in the culture. We also wanted to see how the media take certain themes as important, and, in this case, examine coverage about the public relations event called NetDay.

We began with a discussion of partnerships between business and the nonprofit sector as a common public relations strategy. The case at hand is the partnership called Mass Networks Education Partnership, whose goal is to win wider acceptance of the Internet.

The intent was to deconstruct the public relations campaign from a cultural studies perspective. As stated before, cultural studies is a way to look at media in order to discern the voices that are not heard, and to point out the control and dominance of one voice over others. This is a critical theory through which one might also look at public relations practice.

To explore the campaign we asked questions about the promotional materials from the organization as well as the media coverage of NetDay. The text of the campaign was discussed in the light of a wider economic and political context. In this case, that meant looking at the history of social criticism of technology. Also, through the new technology index we saw how the history of both TV and cable developed along commercial lines, which also seems to be the case with the Internet.

Media coverage of NetDay encodes the importance of the Internet for the twenty-first century, especially for education. Yet, as we have shown, this is the voice of the public relations strategy of the computer industry that the media has assumed, thus becoming almost a spokesperson for the industry. And so the high-tech industry shows its persuasive and economic power to spread its ideas and values into the culture.

A question that we raised here concerned where are the silent voices on the social value of the Internet. They will not be heard from Mass Networks, whose board of directors and funding come from the computer industry. Yet, as a democracy, we need a dissenting voice.

If we hear only the voice of the computer industry, we are set to repeat the stories of TV and cable. The promise of these technologies was hope for greater human compassion and a closer community. It didn't happen. Corporations grew around the industries, producing, marketing, and selling not only programming but also an endless stream of consumer goods. By understanding the history of communication technology, we might see ourselves at a crossroads with the Internet. Will we let the commercial interests of the computer industry dictate the direction of the Internet? Or will we insist that the Internet provide the means to build a stronger local community? That is up to us.

In an effort to maintain national identity, France has voiced opposition to the Internet. We will hear from others. Let them speak.

This chapter set out to examine critically the ideology of a public relations text for the Internet. What is left now is to track the public relations efforts for the dissenting voices about the new technology. Who will provide those voices? Where will we hear or read about them? They are out there. We need to support them so that we can facilitate a dialogue about the Internet technology and not simply accept the voice of the computer industry as the only voice on this issue.

REFERENCES

Andersen, R. (1995). *Consumer culture and TV programming*. Boulder, CO: Westview.

Baker, C. E. (1996). *Advertising and a democratic process*. Princeton, NJ: Princeton University Press.

Bird, E. (1997, March 31). *Cultural studies and TV.* An e-mail message to a cultural studies interest group.

Business group plans $5M drive to counter EPA on environment. (1997, February). *O'Dwyer's Report*, p. 1.

Clinton, Gore push Internet link with schools. (1997, April 20). *Boston Globe*, p. A4.

Conrades, G. (1997, March 11). *The Internet: Where do we go from here?* A speech given at the Network Outlook Conference, hosted by Technologic Partners, San Francisco. http://www.bbn.com/features/businesses/networld.html

Doheny-Farina, S. (1996). *Wired neighborhood*. New Haven, CT: Yale University Press.

Ehrenreich, B. (1995, December 4). Media matters. *The Nation*, p. 698.

End of voluntary ban on TV liquor ads worries PR firms. (1997, March). *O'Dwyer's Report*, p. 1.

Fisher, D. E., & Fisher, M. J. (1996). *Tube: The invention of television*. Washington, DC: Counterpoint.

Gelernter, D. (1996, November 29). Why the Internet should not be an academic topic (letters to the editor). *The Chronicle of Higher Education*, p. B7.

Goldman, R. (1992). *Reading ads socially*. London: Routledge.

Hirston-Shea, D., & Benoit, W. L. (1996, November). *Doonesbury versus the Tobacco Industry: The Smoke Starters Coupon*. A presentation made at the annual meeting of the Speech Communication Association, San Diego.

Innis, H. A. (1972). *Empire and communications*. Toronto: University of Toronto Press.

Leading companies turn to trade associations for lobbying. (1994). *Public Relations Journal, 50*, 13.

Loupe, D. (1996, October 25). Companies pitch in to put schools online. *Atlanta Constitution*, p. C1.

Mass Networks Partnership. (1997a). Promotional material available on the Internet.

Mass Networks Partnership. (1997b). Interview with David Mordecai, project director.

McCarthy, C. (1996, September 10). Computers don't make school user-friendly. *Washington Post*, Sec. C, p. 13.

Mueller, H. J. (1970). *The children of Frankenstein: A primer on modern technology and human values*. Bloomington: Indiana University Press.

Nelson, C., Treichler, P. A., & Grossberg, L. (1992). Cultural studies: An introduction. In L. Grosberg, P. A. Treichler, & C. Nelson (Eds.), *Cultural studies* (pp. 17–22). New York: Routledge.

Ong, W. J. (1982). *Orality and literacy: The technologizing of the word*. London: Methuen.

Postman, N. (1993). *Technopoly: The surrender of culture to technology*. New York: Vintage.

Snyder, L. B. (1996). Technology transfer through cautious eyes. *Journal of Communication, 46*(3), 183–192.

Talk from the Top: 1987 was a very good year for Julie Davis Salisbury (1997, April). *Public Relations Tactics*, pp. 30, 31.

Webb, E. J., Campbell, D. T., Schwartz, R. D., & Sechrest, L. (1972). *Unobtrusive measures: Nonreactive research in the social sciences*. Chicago: Rand McNally.

Wilcox, D. L., Ault, P. H., & Agee, W. K. (1995). *Public relations strategies and tactics* (4th ed.). New York: HarperCollins.

ENDNOTE

[1]Reprinted from *Public Relations Review*, (Vol. 24, 3) T. J. Mickey, "Selling the Internet," pp. 335–349, copyright © 1998, with permission of Elsevier Science.

CHAPTER SIX

Garden According to Martha Stewart

Every other Wednesday in the mid-90s Martha Stewart appeared on the NBC "Today" show without pay, as a promotion for the upcoming issue of her magazine *Martha Stewart Living*. Each topic of discussion came from the magazine (Kasindorf, 1995). Such an appearance is an example of public relations as product promotion or planned communication to sell a product, which, in this case, was a magazine. Although this kind of link between a news/talk show and public relations is becoming more commonplace (Anderson, 1995), the concern in this chapter is with a topic Stewart frequently mentioned on the program and in the magazine: gardening.

As discussed in chapter 4, gardening is the most popular U.S. leisure activity. Eighty percent of American households participate in some gardening activity (Foster, 1994a). Martha Stewart often devotes a section of her magazine and her daily TV program to gardening. About 20% of her magazine editorial content covers gardening.[1] As a media symbol and gardening expert, however, Martha Stewart sells more than gardening when she writes and talks on the subject.

This chapter looks at the production of class by Martha Stewart, particularly through her magazine, *Martha Stewart Living (MSL)*. The central idea is that consumer home and garden magazines, like *MSL*, code and represent class. As a cultural product, they define the upper class so that leisure, for example, for the upper class is connected with flower gardening, whereas leisure for the blue-collar worker is more connected to vegetable gardening.

This chapter is a critical analysis of a public relations text.

The history of gardening gives some insight on how a culture expresses itself through the uses of landscape, especially planting flowers and vegetables in the garden. For example, consumers in their 40s and early 50s—who have more time to spend at home and more discretionary income—have been fertilizing a double-digit spurt in the $26 million gardening industry for the past few years.(Cassidy, 1995). There are some critics of such interest in gardening today, like veteran gardener/journalist James O'Leary (1993), who argued, "Many people still garden for pleasure but I've found that this up-market group has brought the same preoccupation with making money in the 80s to growing things in the 90s—turning a gentle occupation into an all-out obsession. Their gardening is not for themselves but to impress their neighbors, just another accomplishment to be displayed together with the big house and the fine cars." What O'Leary hinted at in his *Newsweek* editorial was that gardening is a statement of class; it is no longer a leisure activity.

Defining gardening and home landscape as class difference is not new. This chapter examines gardening in its social context rather than as an individual activity. How we define "gardening," as we define so many other things, often comes from the media. Therefore, the focus here is on a media text and how it means "gardening."

The problem to be studied can be stated as follows: *Martha Stewart Living* defines gardening as a cultural product produced by both modern publicity and mass consumption to construct and designate class and power. The purpose of this chapter is to look at product promotion as a cultural artifact: Much as hula hoops were in the 1950s, gardening magazines, like *MSL*, are mass-produced vehicles catering to consumer needs and wants today. But in defining consumers' needs, the product promoters also establish class distinction and class values.

The major research questions are: How can we understand the promotion of a magazine as a promotion of class differences? What is the cultural definition of gardening, and what is its significance for power in our culture? How does a public relations text define gardening?

The minor research question is: How can cultural studies contribute to public relations critical theory? There is growing interest in looking at media products from the cultural studies perspective in order to begin to establish a more self-motivated way of life (i.e., one that is less consumer centered and product driven). Many people seek a way of life in which one's value as a person is determined not by how much you own, but by what you contribute toward society's well-being.. Public relations today needs to be open to a critical perspective, perhaps because, according to Schumacher (1980), the great bulk of product promotion is the stimulation of greed, envy, and avarice.

The secondary sources used here include studies on the history of gardening, current surveys of gardening in this country, and the demographics of the magazine in question, *Martha Stewart Living*. As a cultural studies project, this chapter is a study of culture and communication. Williams (1991) distinguished between *object* and *practice* in studying culture. The object is the product; the practice is the environment in which the product is developed. New practices, new meanings, and new values are continually being produced in a culture. We are interested in a particular practice in our culture called gardening, and how that practice is communicated to members of the culture (i.e., how a culture takes as given or natural a kind of practice). Williams noted that in cultural analysis we should look not for the components of a product but for the conditions of a practice. We have to break from the common procedure of isolating the object (e.g., a text) and then discovering its components. On the contrary, we have to discover the nature of a practice and then its condition. Therefore, this chapter looks at the nature of gardening as encoded in a particular meaning for the culture.

In any culture, the refinement of the cultural landscape into gardens always evolves when a given society has time, energy, and desire for more than the merely utilitarian. Going beyond vegetable plots and orchards, gardens can assume an aesthetic dimension: They are relished for their beauty.

Anderson (1972) argued that gardens serve utilitarian as well as aesthetic purposes, but are also an important mode of social communication in the culture. The garden reveals a number of cultural and socioeconomic characteristics (e.g., community affiliation, class, and income) and also reflect the ethnic and regional background of its owner. Anderson's study asserted that the *practice* of gardening is what gives meaning to the *object* of gardening.

Gudowska (1980) discussed the symbolic elements in the use of space in the garden, especially in the Japanese garden. Gudowska examined the use of water, stones, lanterns, and plantings in terms of their new significance for Western architecture.

McIntosh and Shifflett (1982) looked at the two reasons why the elderly choose vegetable gardening: for leisure activity and as dietary supplement. They concluded that the practice is not like other leisure activities and, at the same time, there is little consequence for dietary needs.

Dubost (1983) compared gardening to architecture. The emergence of landscape design was analyzed with a focus on its social and artistic content. Designing a garden has great similarity to designing a building: professional training and art form as well as social status and prestige of the practice. Gardening becomes an art form in a culture through the landscaper, especially when he/she is legitimized as a professional.

Martin (1983) described the first efforts by upper-class residents of Virginia to create formally landscaped gardens on their estates. His focus on class and status made the garden a symbol for cultural capital.

Bradbury (1984) traced the elimination of gardening for the working class in early industrial capitalism when people moved to Montreal from 1861 through 1871. To understand the family economy of the working class in this period, it is necessary to go beyond a simple consideration of the sufficiency of wages and look at nonwage survival strategies like gardening as a source of revenue and self-worth for those who relocated to Montreal.

Looking at gardening how-to books from 1900 through 1937, Seaton (1985) concluded that as farming waned the middle class rose, and having a well-tended flower and vegetable garden became an essential aspect of ideal family life.

In the United States, a social movement of gardening was proposed by the government for certain cities but was also carried out by urban garden collectives. Jamison (1985) examined how different meanings of gardening that came from the government bureaucracies and the collectives often produced conflict. Agencies and collectives had views of reality and distinct meanings both for the "joys" and activity of gardening and for gardeners themselves.

Cleveland and Soleri (1987) discussed the differences between household gardening and industrial gardens, especially as they impact Third-World nations. The two forms have different goals and different means: One has technology, speed, and science; and the other has leisure, additional household income, and increased status for women. There may be many valid reasons why households do not have gardens, or do not have bigger or different gardens. In any attempt to improve productivity, nutritional status, or increased income of households through gardens, the evidence suggests the necessity of analyzing the internal dynamics of both garden and household; the relationship between the two; and the relationship of both with external social, economic, political, and environmental forces that determine the household's control over resources for and production from gardens.

In all of these studies, what becomes clear is that gardening is viewed as a cultural practice in the context of the economic and political issues at stake. The meaning of gardening for a culture is created by the consciousness-producing organizations in the culture, especially government, businesses, and the media.

Public relations is managed communication to impact a particular public about a product or service. Habermas (1991) called for critical theory to examine public relations practice because the public sphere that formerly emerged from society is now being produced by public relations personnel. Ideas in the public forum are being generated by public relations practitioners for the private good of their organizations.

McDonald (1995) examined an extensive amount of public relations research and concluded that critical research is practically nonexistent. This is an area that public relations researchers need to address.

German (1995) maintained that critical theory means raising the values located in messages to the status of observable objects, which then become the focus of reflection and criticism. She argued for public relations critical theory in order to assess the functioning of language and reconstructing the prevailing understandings that are shared among individuals but taken for granted by those individuals. The question posed by all critical theory addresses the balance of power in public dialogue.

This chapter looks at the promotion of gardening as a practice, especially through the promotion of the magazine *Martha Stewart Living*. Martha Stewart herself is an organization and a symbol of consumer culture; she is not simply a private person. That makes her self-promotion and the promotion of her magazine ideal for public relations critical inquiry. The goal is to deconstruct the public relations text in the magazine *Martha Stewart Living*.

Social theorist Pierre Bourdieu (1984) talked about cultural products as a source of power in a culture, and how they become a social artifact for designating class. The product (the magazine *MSL*) and the promotion of Martha Stewart together promote a form of gardening that constructs class distinction. Bourdieu is the major theorist we use to help understand the production of class through the symbol of gardening.

In his work, Bourdieu explored the social and economic origins of cultural taste. He questioned the relative autonomy of culture that is used by unjust social systems to reproduce themselves, even against the self-interest of large segments of the population. He provided a critical voice for a sociology of culture, and used the materiality of text to make his argument.

Bourdieu (1991) wrote about sports, which one could compare to gardening insofar as both are cultural expressions. He noted:

> An explanatory model capable of accounting for the distribution of sporting [gardening] practices among the classes and class fractions must clearly take account of the positive or negative determining factors, the most important of which are *spare time* (a transformed form of economic capital), *economic time* (more or less indispensable depending on the sport [type of gardening]), and *cultural capital* (again, more or less depending on the sport [type of gardening]). (p. 367)

The three meanings of time (spare, cultural, and economic) all can apply as well to the practice of gardening as they do to sports. A look at gardening must take into consideration how different classes make use of time to create the meaning that they give to gardening. Gardening thus can become a way to understand class, and the promotion of gardening can become a way to produce class.

Using the cultural and class symbol of sport, Bourdieu (1991) said:

> The probability of practicing the different sports [types of gardening] depends, to a different degree for each sport, primarily on economic capital and secondarily on cultural capital and spare time; it also depends on the affinity between the ethical and aesthetic dispositions characteristic of each class or class faction and the objective potentialities of ethical or aesthetic accomplishment which are or seem to be contained in each sport [type of gardening]. (p. 369)

Featherstone (1987) criticized the view of "lifestyle" so current in market research. He maintained that in using Bourdieu's social theory, rather than an image of consumer culture based on choice and individualization, lifestyle and consumption are totally manipulated by capitalist mass society. What is consumed is not something useful so much as signs. The signs become what is associated with power in the culture. Thus, class status becomes aligned with cultural signs, which can include the garden. Along the same line of thought, and quoting Bourdieu, Wilson (1988) described a model of social action in which people internalize objective structures and rearticulate them as free choices.

Min (1992) noted that, in the field of communication, the political economy emphasizes the direct relations between cultural texts and socioeconomic realities. He used Bourdieu to show how cultural forms are an expression of the structure of domination in society. A systematic study of the cultural forms in which this domination is revealed illustrates the way of life of different classes.

The basic notion in Bourdieu's methodological position is his conception of the *habitus*. Bourdieu (1979) defined it as a "system of durable, transposable dispositions which functions as the generative basis of structured, objectively unified practices" (p. 92). There is a cultural code that defines a symbolic value to cultural practices, and the habitus of each group or class is formed in the practical choice of utilizing these values.

The notion of *capital* is the crux of Bourdieu's class theory. *Cultural capital* refers to cultural knowledge as a resource of power used by individuals and social groups to improve their positions within the social class structure (Bourdieu, 1977). *Economic capital* refers to monetary assets that can be accumulated and invested as part of class strategy. Cultural capital is harder to measure than economic capital is because there is no clear equivalent to the medium of money in the sphere of culture. For Bourdieu, cultural capital is the incorporation of symbolic, cognitive, and aesthetic competencies via implicit learning processes mainly within the family socialization. The acquisition of cultural capital in the sense of incorporation is the prerequisite for the possibility of symbolically appropriating that cultural capital as objectified in cultural goods like artifacts, books, pictures, and so on (and may even include a gardening magazine like *MSL*; Bourdieu, 1984).

Bourdieu believed that the systems of domination persist and reproduce themselves without conscious recognition by a society's members. Although Bourdieu concentrated his attention on the model of domination—on what he called the exercise of symbolic power[2]—his theory, according to Garnham and Williams (1986), is cast in materialist terms. Bourdieu used the terms—borrowed from economics and including *capital*, *profit*, *market* and *investment*—to describe and analyze cultural practice. His theory seeks an analysis of the mode of production of material life.

MacLean (1993) gave credit to Bourdieu for taking a holistic approach to culture that transcends the objective/subjective dichotomy to unmask the alleged "disinterestedness" of a cultural form. The producer of a media text is not just photographing or writing, but is materializing the values and ideology of the time.

This chapter uses the lens of cultural studies to look at the cultural artifacts of words and images about gardening. Nelson, Treichler, and Grossberg (1992) maintained that, in the cultural studies tradition, culture is understood both as a way of life (encompassing ideas, attitudes, languages, practices, institutions, and structures of power) and as a whole range of cultural practices (artistic forms, texts, canons, architecture, mass-produced commodities, etc.). The objective of looking at the culture from a cultural studies perspective is to point out the inequalities and the oppression of any minority voice. Therefore, cultural studies is not simply a glimpse at pop culture but rather an investigation of political and economic hegemony.

Although to date not much public relations critical work has been subjected to cultural studies analysis, it is a possible way to look at product promotion. This is because, in a consumer culture, any product or service becomes a media product as well, through such planned communication forms as public relations campaigns. This is the case with the form of gardening promoted by *MSL*.

Nelson et al. (1992) argued that all forms of cultural production need to be studied in relation to other cultural practices and in the context of their social and historical structures. Cultural studies is thus committed to the study of the text in relation to the entire range of a society's arts, beliefs, institutions, and communicative practices.

Ang (1993) noted that it is important for cultural studies to pay attention to the particular historical conditions and the specific trajectories through which actual social subjects become both different and similar. Categories like class and gender are therefore important areas of investigation.

The cultural studies perspective looks at a cultural product as a way to understand the distribution of power and ideology. Cultural studies requires us to identify the operation of specific practices, of how they continuously reinscribe the line between legitimate and popular culture, and of what they accomplish in specific contexts.

Any method of cultural studies analysis must therefore identify the operation of specific practices. For example, one must know something about the practice of gardening in the culture. How actors of different social and economic status deal with gardening is important. Also, one must look at the construction of gardening in media forms that promote gardening, like the *MSL* magazine. Gardening as a form of cultural expression exists within a certain context of class and power, and serves certain social purposes. Bourdieu's sociology of culture helps deconstruct the public relations text in that context.

Golding and Murdock (1978) challenged the researcher who uses a cultural studies approach. They argued that to say that the mass media are saturated with bourgeois ideology is simply to pose a series of questions for investigation. To begin to answer them, however, it is necessary to go on to show how this hegemony is actually produced through the concrete activities of the media personnel and the interpreting procedures of consumers. This requires detailed and direct analysis of the *social context* of production and reception, and their relations to the central institutions and processes of class societies. Extrapolations from cultural texts, no matter how subtle and elaborate, are no substitute.

To illustrate an exceptional use of *textual analysis* as a cultural studies method, one could look at Berger (1991). He showed how photographs from the turn of the twentieth century can give us a superb insight into class and difference as constructed by the culture.

Peza (1993) argued for an examination of the text as well as the reader in a cultural and mass media context. This *MSL* project attempts to do both.

Finally, German (1995), in discussing public relations critical inquiry, asked the researcher to consider not only the *propositional* function of a message (the information, the text) but also the *performative* function (who we are in relation to the text). Spokespersons for the organization, including public relations practitioners, have an impact beyond making a profit. German asserted that they create culture. As a result, public relations does not just contribute messages and products to the public dialogue, but it also creates relationships in society that hold consequences for the evolution of society.

It is appropriate to examine communication and culture through Martha Stewart herself as a text because her magazine, like all her projects, is commercially driven. Green (1995) said that, like Ralph Lauren and Calvin Klein, the New Jersey-born Stewart has built an empire based on packaging a distinctive take on American style. "I'm a brand," Martha proudly says. She is at the helm of a company with its own publishing, TV, interactive media, and merchandising projects. Therefore, Martha's view of gardening[3] is readily available as a prominent media text.

The major research statement for this chapter is that *Martha Stewart Living* defines gardening as a cultural product produced by both modern publicity and mass consumption to construct and designate class and power. The method to examine this statement includes two steps. First is a textual analysis or an examination of the media text. The text includes a series of photos of gardening from *MSL*. Second, in order to make sense of the text, we must look at the following as well:

1. The demographics of the magazine *MSL*.
2. Surveys from the National Gardening Association.
3. Current trends in gardening according to the popular press.

A definition of the terms and concepts is important before continuing. *Gardening* is the choice and placement of plant material and structures by the homeowner. *Cultural product* is an expression in a mass-produced, material form, usually tied to an art form, from an organization (whose objective is economic profit within a particular culture) to a public. *Modern publicity* is the public relations use of planned communication to specific audiences usually by means of media technology, including the Internet, in order to increase the sales of any service or product. *Mass consumption* means that the end result of the media campaign is that large numbers of individuals in the culture purchase and/or make use of the product or service for their own needs, which often originate in the words and images of the public relations material from the organization. *Class division* means that the population is distinguished by social parameters such as economic status, education, employment, and use of art. *Power* is control over some ideology in the culture.

Martha Stewart Living magazine has been published since 1991. The magazine reaches 3,640,000 adults.[4] The editorial department of *MSL* offers its philosophy for covering the topic of gardening in these words: "Martha shares her expertise in growing beautiful things, from summer and fall to winter and spring. Complete information for making your garden as personal and beautiful as possible, whether your plot encompasses acres of land or terra-cotta pots."[5]

The topic of gardening is offered in almost every issue of the magazine. Accompanying every article on gardening are always some photographs. Because photographs are intended to accent the article, one might study the photos as a way to understand the philosophy or value system incorporated in the text. That is what we do next.

Five photos are discussed here. Each of them accompanies an article on gardening. These photos were chosen as representative of pictures from articles on gardening over a 2-year period. The issues of the magazine in which these photos appeared were published in the months from March till October, when most articles on gardening generally appear.

In the first photo, we see a New England fence in an early morning view. There are tall evergreen trees in the background in addition to the grass and the fence that give context to the flowers. These flowers are housed in an upper-class setting, which is probably a mansion or an estate.

Several small photos that accompany an article about arranging rows of flowers and vegetables appear in another larger photo. The top left photo shows several long rows lined with string, where plantings are to be put. There are large trees and trellises at the top of the row. These give the reader the idea of an opulence and upper-class status that must accompany anyone who could afford this much land. In the photo of the lower row and on the left, you can see Martha herself working with her head gardener. How many people can afford a head gardener? The kind of project she outlined here probably demands the help of a gardener.

A third photo features an image of a semishady "moon garden" in Washington Depot, Connecticut, where in 1996 the average home price was $280,349 and the average family income was $51,532.[6] There is also an iron-rod bench on the right, with a bird feeder in front. This is a well-cultivated, white garden and probably not something for the working class in this country, but more for the upper class. Living in this town in Connecticut is certainly not affordable on the average income of a blue-collar worker.

Wave Hill, a public garden in New York City, is shown in the next photo. The focus of the photo is a pot garden under a pergola. This is from an era of early twentieth-century opulence when people donated large sums of money to have lush but extravagant displays of plants in a setting that offered refuge to the weary city dweller who could come and gaze, but not own. The benefactors were usually wealthy capitalists who had little connection with the working class but wanted to have their wealth on display.

Finally, a garden about to awaken in the spring is shown in the fifth photo. But where is the garden? It is on at least an acre of land, with the main house in the background and another building on the far right. There are also very tall trees on the property. The setting gives the impression of wealth and social standing. There is a great need for garden help here because there are so many beds of flowers and other plants. This is probably not the home of a middle-class laborer but rather of a professional who can afford to hire extensive garden help.

In all the photos used here the focus is on wealthy, upper-class, suburban gardeners as reflected and produced in the pages of *MSL*. The lower class, working class, and even the middle class can only dream of being part of this kind of gardening. It is a gardening framed, represented, and promoted as upper class and for the wealthy. Such seems to be the kind of gardening presented by *MSL*.

The magazine made its readership profile available. Notice in Table 6.1 the comparisons of the *MSL* readership with 1995 U.S. government statistics.[7]

The audience for the magazine is wealthier than is the average American. More of the magazine's readers are in professional and management positions. Almost all of the *MSL* readers are college graduates, which is quite different from the American population as a whole, among whom only 22% are college educated.

What these numbers indicate is that the image of gardening from the magazine is constructed to designate class and power. The class is an upper class, and the power is one based on economics. Readers have the house and garden as well as the income to do the kind of gardening that Martha proposes. Martha Stewart defines gardening as a cultural product through publicity, and

TABLE 6.1
***MSL* Profile**

	Martha Stewart Living	*U.S. Government Statistics*
	Readership	
Median household income	$56,821	$31,241
Percentage professional/managerial	33%	23%
Percentage college educated	73%	22%

makes it possible through mass consumption. She produces a particular form of gardening and therefore, because of her mass marketing, exhibits a certain kind of hegemony in regard to this cultural expression. Thus, for many people, to have a garden is to have a Martha Stewart kind of garden.

The National Gardening Survey is conducted annually by the National Gardening Association. The information that follows is from their 1993–94 survey.[8] The demographic group rated highest on the lawn and garden participation index were college educated, professional/business people, and households with annual incomes of $50,000 or more (National Gardening Association, 1993). The index rates demographic groups in the U.S. household population according to their involvement in lawn and garden activities.

Flower gardening was most popular with people 30 years of age and older, in college-educated households, among people with professional or business occupations, and in households with annual incomes of more than $75,000.

On the other hand, there were more households of manual labor occupations with vegetable gardens than any other group. The household income was $30,000 or more.

According to this survey, the richer and more educated you are, the more likely you are to plant flowers. More blue-collar gardeners have vegetable gardens. These data clearly point out some class differences in garden practices. The *MSL* reader/gardener is more likely to be in the flower gardening group, because flower gardening is more of an upper-class practice.

Seventy-one percent of U.S. households participate in lawn and garden activities. The signs of power and wealth in our culture as they relate to gardening as a cultural symbol clearly are a class-related practice of gardening. That class is wealthier and more educated than that which defines gardening as a vegetable plot. If you garden, and the majority of people in this country do, that practice is related to class.

For those who are into gardening, it is important to get information to keep up to date about trends in gardening. Gardening information is purchased by 19% of households. The most important consumers of gardening information are college-educated professionals with annual incomes of $40,000 and more. Information frequently comes from gardening magazines (National Gardening Association, 1993).

Foster (1994b) noted that 28 new garden magazines appeared on the newsstand between 1987 and 1994. Nine new periodicals were unveiled in 1993 alone. Foster commented, "The forty-something generation has flocked to the garden like worms to compost. With their yen for stylish pots and fashionable fencing, they have driven gardening to startling highs" (p. 1).

Carmody (1995) asserted that after baby boomers put finishing touches on the inside of their houses, the logical place for them to turn their attention to is the outside. To fill the need for gardening information, more magazines arrived on the scene. She noted, for example, that *Garden Design* readers have a household income of $71,000 and *Home Garden* readers an income of $57,000.

The media product called "gardening magazine" has been a way for the upscale gardener to satisfy his/her need for information. What the magazines, most like *MSL*, also indicate is that gardening is a class-defining practice. If you are upper class, you do fine gardening, and it's no coincidence that those two words are the name of yet another upscale magazine, *Fine Gardening*.

This discussion has shown the link between *MSL*'s version of gardening and class. *MSL* promotes a form of gardening intended for an upper class that is wealthy, highly educated, and professional. This is consumer-driven gardening.

Gardens are an important form of social communication in the culture. The garden reveals cultural status.

We are not just discussing gardening but *a kind of gardening*, produced in this case by *MSL* as a public relations text. Although every culture defines what gardening is to mean, it is the job of the social critic to point out *whose* meaning is promoted. Gardening today is gardening according to the media, and that means upper-class and status-promoting gardening.

Where are the days when we gardened for leisure? That does not seem to be the case today.

Martha Stewart produces her product of style in home and garden with a certain consumer mentality. She has said, "We dissected the business in four main divisions: publishing, television, multi-media and merchandising. And we talked about how you take over an area—in my case, the home, the garden, the surroundings—and monopolize it" (as quoted in Kasindorf, 1995, p. 31).

It is important to look at Martha's media promotion critically, as we did here, in order to raise awareness of the kind of cultural values being proposed. Martha Stewart equates gardening (she would include everything connected with home and garden) with wealth and class. Who says that is gardening? Where is the balance of voices here? Where is the balance of power? Where is another definition of gardening being presented? These are the questions raised in public relations deconstruction: a critique of product promotion as public relations practice.

Martha Stewart, to paraphrase Bourdieu, is reproducing herself in her definition of gardening. But what about the self-interests of other segments of the population?

Some may say we are only talking about gardening, not nuclear defense, but media promotion like that of Martha Stewart has an influence on the cultural definition of a practice like gardening. People internalize objective structures like media promotional material, and rearticulate them as free choices. That is a form of domination of the media that needs to be questioned. Where is freedom if all you can express is what the media says?

Cultural forms like *MSL* are an example of the structure of domination in society, and illustrate the construction of difference in classes. Gardening, for the upper class, becomes cultural capital—a way to improve one's position within the social class structure. Members of that class want more and more of the kind of sign value of gardening produced by *MSL*.

The social environment has produced several publications on gardening that take the same focus as *MSL*. Systems of domination persist and reproduce themselves without conscious recognition by society's members; and so we see more and more of the same type of gardening magazine.

Aesthetics, like gardening as art form, are prone to class interests. The sign of class status in this project is *MSL* and Martha Stewart. What is so alarming is that the subject—gardening—seems so innocuous, yet it is a source of power for those who define it for the rest of us.

In June 1996, Martha appeared on the "Today" show to talk about shade gardening. She had created a small, temporary garden site outside the NBC studio in Rockefeller Center. She had pots of plants, rocks, and soil arranged as if in a shady woodland area. It appeared to be quite the feat for her assistants to set up. That same week her magazine appeared on the newsstands. In the magazine was an article about shade gardening, making the NBC event another example of the Grande Dame of self-promotion as she gets one more foothold in the American psyche and one step closer toward her dream of defining taste for all of us.

That is precisely the issue here.

Public relations, defined as product promotion, is not only about promoting products like gardening tools, magazines, paint, and so on; public relations is also about drowning out opposing voices or attempting to make your voice the only one heard. That is why Habermas critiqued public relations in contemporary society: It is constructed for economic reasons and not democratic reasons.

The fact that today there is so much oppositional reading of Martha is quite significant. Several journalists have criticized Martha as the "too"-perfect hostess. There is a book entitled *Is Martha Stewart Living?* Also, there is a one-woman play on a similar theme. These are readers who reject Martha's version of home and garden. That action ought to be welcomed in a democracy. When we see someone like Martha, who wants to become a voice for class and style and works so hard to do it, we ask, "What class? Whose style?" Her use of print, TV, and interactive media to get her message out there is not just great business sense, it is also an example of public relations that has become inserted into everyday media, especially news stories. How often do we pick up a paper and not know that the source of the story is a public relations practitioner? That is the point of this chapter: to make us aware that public relations practice promotes more than a product or service. Public relations constructs cultural differences.

REFERENCES

Anderson, E. N. (1972). On the folk art of landscaping. *Western Folklore, 31*(3), 179–188.

Anderson, R. (1995). *Consumer culture and tv programming*. Boulder, CO: Westview.

Ang, I. (1993). To be or not to be Chinese: Diaspora, culture, and postmodern ethnicity. *Southeast Asian Journal of Social Science, 21*(1), 1–17.

Berger, J. (1991). The suit and the photograph. In C. Mukerji & M. Schudson (Eds.), *Rethinking popular culture: Contemporary perspectives in cultural studies* (pp. 424–431). Berkeley: University of California Press.

Bourdieu, P. (1977). *Outline of a theory of practice*. (R. Nice, Trans.). Cambridge, UK: Cambridge University Press.

Bourdieu, P. (1979). *Algeria 1960*. Cambridge, UK: Cambridge University Press.

Bourdieu, P. (1984). *Distinction*. Cambridge, MA: Harvard University Press.

Bourdieu, P. (1991). Sport and social class. In C. Mukerji & M. Schudson (Eds.), *Rethinking popular culture: Contemporary perspectives in cultural studies* (pp. 357–373). Berkeley: University of California Press.

Bradbury, B. (1984). Pigs, cows, and boarders: Non-wage forms of survival among Montreal families, 1861–1891. *Labour* (Canada), *14*, 9–46.

Carmody, D. (1995, Feb. 6). Magazines follow bay boomers into the garden. *New York Times*, p. D6.

Cassidy, T. (1995, Aug. 21). A boom in blooms: Gardening industries gain as baby boomers' interests grow. *Boston Globe*, p. 21.

Cleveland, D., & Soleri, D. (1987). Household gardens as a development strategy. *Human Organization, 46*(3), 259–267.

Dubost, F. (1983). Landscape designers and the invention of landscape. *Sociologie-du-Travail, 25*(4), 432–445.

Featherstone, M. (1987). Lifestyle and consumer culture. *Theory, Culture, and Society, 4*(1), 55–70.

Foster, M. (1994b, May 20). Boomers bring a bumper crop of new publications. *Atlantic Journal and Constitution*, p. F1.

Foster, M. (1994a, April 9). It's hoe, hoe, hoe all the way to the bank for the garden industry. *Atlanta Journal and Constitution*, p. B1.

Garnham, N., & Williams, R. (1986). Pierre Bourdieu and sociology of culture. In P. Collins et al. (Eds.), *Media, culture, and society* (pp. 116–130). Beverly Hills, CA: Sage.

German, K. M. (1995). Critical theory in public relations inquiry. In W. N. Elwood (Ed.), *Public relations inquiry as rhetorical criticism* (pp. 279–294). Westport, CT: Praeger.

Golding, P., & Murdock, G. (1978). Theories of communication—theories of society. *Communication Research, 5*, 339–356.

Green, M. (1995, Oct. 2). The best revenge. *People*, pp. 101–110.

Gudowska, I. (1980). Garden art of Japan; Ogrody Japonii. *Prezeeglad-Socjologiczny, 32*(I), 197–221.

Habermas, J. (1991). The public sphere. In C. Mukerji & M. Schudson (Eds.), *Rethinking popular culture: Contemporary perspectives in cultural studies* (pp. 398–404). Berkeley: University of California Press.

Jamison, M. S. (1985). The joys of gardening: Collectivist and bureaucratic cultures in conflict. *The Sociological Quarterly, 26*(4), 473–490.

Kasindorf, J. R. (1995, June). Martha, Inc. *Working Woman*, pp. 26–31, 66–69.

Landscape as art. (1994). *Collier's Encyclopedia*, p. 290. New York: Collier.

MacLean, I. (1993). Bourdieu's field of cultural production. *French Cultural Studies, 4*(3), 283–289.

Martin, P. (1983). Long and assiduous endeavors: Gardening in early eighteenth-century Virginia. *Eighteenth-Century Life, 8*(2), 107–116.

McDonald, B. (1995, Nov.). *Public relations agenda*. Presentation given at the Speech Communication Association annual meeting, San Antonio, TX.

McIntosh, W., & Shifflett, P. (1982). *Vegetable gardening as leisure or as dietary supplement*. A paper presented at the Rural Sociological Society meeting.

Min, E. J. (1992, Nov.). Can political economy of communication be incorporated with cultural studies in postmodern era? *Viewpoints, 120, Information Analyses (070)*, 1–28

National Gardening Association. (1993). *The National Gardening Survey 1993–1994*. Burlington, VT: Author.

Nelson C., Treichler, P., & Grossberg, L. (1992). Cultural studies: An introduction. In L. Grossberg, C. Nelson, & P. Treichler (Eds.), *Cultural studies* (pp. 1–17). New York: Routledge.

O'Leary, J. V. (1993, April 19). What would Virgil say? *Newsweek*, p. 18.

Peza, C. (1993). The interminable reader: An approach to the study of reception. *Version-Estudies de Communication y Politica, 3*, 57–82.

Schumacher, E. F. (1980). *Good work*. London: Abacus.

Seaton, B. (1985). Gardening books for the commuter's wife, 1900–1937. *Landscape, 28*(2), 41–47.

Williams, R. (1991). Base and superstructure in Marxist cultural theory. In C. Mukerji & M. Schudson (Eds.), *Rethinking popular culture: Contemporary perspectives in cultural studies* (pp. 407–423). Berkeley: University of California Press.

Wilson, E. (1988). Picasso and pae de foise gras: Pierre Bourdieu's sociology of culture. *Diacritics, 18*(2), 47–60.

ENDNOTES

[1]This is from the marketing material sent from the magazine to advertising inquiries. Source: *Hall's Editorial Reports* (1994, Dec.).

[2]Symbolic capital cannot be objectified, institutionalized, or incorporated, because it is dependent on its activation and affirmation by actual communicative practices (Bourdieu, 1984).

[3]Here we are discussing only gardening, although Martha Stewart also discusses other home topics like setting the dinner table, entertaining, painting the house, and so on.

[4]This figure is according to the MRI Fall 1995 survey data supplied by the magazine to potential advertisers.

[5]From the marketing material sent by the magazine to advertising inquiries (Fall 1995).

[6]Information on house and income levels are from the *Connecticut Town Profiles* (1996).

[7]Source is the *Statistical Abstract of the United States 115th Edition* (1995, p. 469).

[8]National Gardening Association. (1993). *The National Gardening Survey 1993–1994*. Burlington, VT: Author. Conducted by the Gallup Organization, Inc.

CHAPTER SEVEN

A Community Relations Campaign

Public relations is defined by Wilcox, Ault, and Agee (1995) as managed communication to create favorable opinion toward an organization. Under this definition, the production of mass media material to persuade an audience often becomes part of an individual public relations campaign.

The field of health care public relations includes communication to get messages out to various publics in order to promote healthy lifestyle choices. The practice could be part of the public relations efforts of a hospital, clinic, or other health organization. In a consumer-driven, capitalist environment like the United States, we also have the private sector, which, as part of its public relations efforts, may provide health-related messages through videos, brochures, and so on. One such corporate community relations campaign is the focus of this chapter.

Flora (1993) noted that health communication needs to use more cultural and critical studies of the media in order to understand the health messages presented in print, video, and films. Most people simply accept media messages concerning health issues as the way health issues actually are. However, the media often present mixed messages on what is healthy. One glaring example is the advertising of sugared cereals to children.

This chapter takes a cultural studies approach to a media product that is part of a community relations program from a major brewery. The research objective is to deconstruct the public relations text. A minor research question is to see how the larger culture helps us make sense of a public relations campaign.

There is a growing interest in the study of media from the cultural studies perspective. Toth and Heath (1992) discussed the importance of a critical theory for public relations. Kellner (1995) maintained that a true cultural studies approach of a media text must align itself with a critical view that looks at the text in the light of its economic and political context.

At the same time, there needs to be more accountability for public relations as a practice. The public interest is at stake. Every public relations campaign needs to be open to a critical view.

Product promotion as both advertising and public relations can often raise questions for the public when the product is a potential health hazard. One must ask the question whether a company that makes a product like cigarettes or alcohol, which present so many health hazards, can conduct a public service campaign. Madden and Grube (1994) examined the message of a public service announcement (PSA) for alcohol that was primarily about abuse prevention. Most often, the theme of such alcohol-related PSAs is preventing underage drinking or drinking and driving. However, we also need to know the values or ideology about health we are producing in the public relations text that we send out. Health messages in any media campaign are understood and criticized in the political, economic, and, in this case, health environment of a given culture.

The ideology of a public service campaign may fail, for example, to show alcohol as a *problem* substance. Instead, alcohol may be represented as a valueless substance whose worth is determined solely by the consumer. That is not the message of health care professionals. A public service campaign from the liquor industry may simply reinforce alcohol as a substance of choice, but a substance nonetheless.

Another example of a problematic public relations text is a campaign by the Dairy Association. Included in one of the association's press kits were several black-and-white photos. The photos showed milk on a table with various snack foods like cake, cookies, and a piece of pie. The intent of the photos was to show how milk could accompany a snack. The message also coming across to the reader is it is all right to eat sugar and fat, which is in all the snacks pictured. Yet, the health community has been telling us that we need to cut down on sugar and fat. In trying to promote milk, the Dairy Association was giving us an unhealthy message.

The larger question in any critical study of public relations practice is to ask how public relations practitioners are held to accountability. The media strategy they apply is produced in a text that becomes part of a culture. Words and images are chosen that will be accepted by the public. It is that text that needs to be open to scrutiny. In this chapter, we examine the ideology of a video that is part of a community relations campaign.

This chapter looks at the Anheuser-Busch community relations campaign called Family Talk, which promotes responsible drinking. Family Talk is a community service campaign that makes its video and other printed material available to anyone who calls an 800 number. In the campaign parents are charged with the responsibility to talk to their children about the issue of responsible drinking. However, what is the ideology on alcohol and drinking in the Family Talk video produced by Anheuser-Busch in this community relations campaign?

The following literature review focuses on three areas: communication and public relations theory, concerns about alcohol and advertising in the media, and abuse prevention models from health care professionals.

Carey (1975) wrote that media is ritual communication for the members of the culture because the media provides a way of understanding ourselves. Therefore, it is crucial to look at the media critically, in order to live in a democratic society.

In public relations practice, the symbols, words, and images of the communication vehicle also communicate the values and ideology of the culture (Altman, 1990). To question the media text is a way to question the values and ideology proposed.

Finn and Strickland (1982) discussed the message of alcohol advertising as one that leads to a state of wellness for the consumer: Just have a drink. Never is any problem about drinking presented.

Grube and Wallack (1994) showed how naturally children seem to accept the alcohol messages in the media. Their knowledge and beliefs about alcohol are formed by the media.

Mosher (1994) pointed out the need to position alcohol as a public health hazard and that it poses a greater risk for some individuals than for others. Therefore, one cannot simply say that the product is neutral and everything depends on how you handle it.

The research of Grube and Wallack (1994) provided support for the hypothesis that awareness of alcohol advertising influences children's drinking beliefs, knowledge, and intentions.

Daugherty and O'Bryan (1987) proposed that the important model of abuse prevention in this country is the lifestyle risk reduction model, not the be responsible model or the how to handle peer pressure model. He traced the history of models of prevention in this country (see Table 7.1). Notice how, from top to bottom, the meanings of alcohol for the culture change.

At the turn of the 20th century the *temperance model* pushed for the elimination of distilled spirits. That social movement had begun in the nineteenth century in various parts of the country. In 1920, the *prohibition model* meant elimination of all alcohol or total abstinence. The temperance movement had achieved its goal, passing a federal law outlawing the harmful substance called alcohol.

The *disease model* discussed prevention and recovery. Alcoholics Anonymous (AA), born in 1935, held that the alcoholic is sick. In 1951, the World Health Organization stated that alcoholism was a disease.

In 1966, the American Medical Association inaugurated the *normative model,* which was designed to normalize the use of alcohol

TABLE 7.1
Models of Abuse Prevention

Temperance model
Prohibition model
Disease model
Normative model
Information model
Developmental model
Responsible decision-making model
Public health model
Peer resistance model
Lifestyle risk reduction model

by making a distinction between appropriate and inappropriate drinking. Norms and laws spell out the way to deal with alcohol.

The *information model* said that people develop alcohol and drug problems out of ignorance. Under this model, if people are given the right information, they will not abuse alcohol. The *developmental model* held that people become drug abusers due to some flaw in their developmental process, such as low self-esteem and poor communication skills.

Then there was the *responsible decision-making model,* which was really phase two of the normative model. The emphasis here was on making responsible choices. Alcohol is a neutral substance. You just have to make the right choice to use it responsibly.

The *public health model* held the view that the primary prevention approach was to control the availability of the substance. The more drinking there is in the general population, the greater the number of people there are who are chronically dependent on alcohol and, therefore, the greater the extent of serious alcohol-related health effects.

Another version of the developmental model was called the *peer resistance model.* Peer pressure was the focus in the early 1980s, and the peer resistance model approach was age sensitive. For example, programs like DARE—which deals with 6th and 7th graders—were started then to help young people resist peer pressure.

Finally, the *lifestyle risk reduction model* insists that health and impairment problems develop as a result of the interaction between biology and the quantity and frequency of alcohol use. This model draws from heart disease research. For example, if someone has a heart condition, he/she should not consume certain foods. Food is not a neutral entity. Certain foods with high fat could kill a person with a heart condition. Special content in an educational program is used to reduce the risk. Learning new skills is important to reduce risk. The same line of thought applies to alcohol. It becomes necessary to separate the use of drugs, including alcohol, for those at risk. Alcohol is the number-one drug in our culture. Alcohol as a drink or as substance is a *problem.*

The research question therefore is as follows: What is the ideology of the community relations campaign video produced by the Anheuser-Busch Corporation? A community relations or public service campaign message encodes the value system and ideology of the organization. The campaign also encodes the values of a culture and becomes the way to think about such issues as the economy, the political environment, or what it means to be healthy. Ritual communication implies that the cultural symbols of word and image, especially media, become the ways we think about ourselves and the world. (Carey, 1975). A public service campaign as ritual communication reinforces certain values and ideology that become what's natural for the society.

The historical background for this chapter rests on two sources: first, the way the health community has addressed alcohol in this country; second, the use of community relations programs from corporations as a way of showing concern to the community. The theory important to this project is the cultural studies approach to popular culture products, including public relations media products.

The *lifestyle risk reduction model* of abuse prevention is the present theory from the field of health promotion on how to address alcohol problems in the society. Yet, the beer industry continues to extol responsible drivers, responsible drinking, bartender training and designated drivers advocation. Such efforts seem to imply that alcohol is not a public health issue, but rather a private matter that can be resolved as long as you control your intake of the substance. There is a conflict of messages here: the brewery message versus the message from the health community. Therefore, the research problem is: What is the relationship between the public relations text and culture?

The method to address the research problem here is a form of cultural analysis called *textual analysis*. Porter (1992) used textual analysis to examine the Mobil public service announcements on the environment. He took a critical view of public relations practice, and showed the need to look at the ideology present in those PSAs. Also, Coffin (1994) examined the ideology of an advertising campaign to sell sewing machines in late nineteenth-century France. The campaign was not only selling machines, but ways to understand gender, age, class, and labor as well.

The process used her is to deconstruct a public service video from Anheuser-Busch called *Family Talk*. The 32-minute video from the public relations campaign is the text. There is also a discussion of the video in relation to the models of abuse prevention from the health community. Finally, a comparison is made between what the video says and what, according to health educators, is the current model of alcohol abuse prevention.

The purpose of the *Family Talk* video was to show parents how to talk to their children about drinking. Children aged 9 to 11 were proposed as the ideal audience.

Two experts introduced on the video were Dr. Lonnie Carton, an education consultant, and Dr. David Ohlms, Medical Director of St. Mary's and St. Joseph's Recovery Center. In the video, Ohlms said, "If children observe responsible drinking by parents, they are not likely to become problem drinkers themselves." The goal of the *Family Talk* program, according to Carton, "is to help parents to stop underage drinking before it starts."

The two models of abuse prevention presented in the video were *be responsible* and *peer versus parent* as source of influence for the child, in which the parent is the stronger role model. The information in the video and in the *Family Talk* printed material that accompanied it was based on input from the Family Talk Advisory Panel, a group of six education and health experts. The panel gave the campaign credibility and was itself also a public relations strategy (Wilcox, Ault, & Agee, 1995).

A theme that ran throughout the video was "Let's stop underage drinking before it starts." Carton provided basic guidelines on how to talk to one's child about drinking. Her guidelines were:

1. Start early. Prime time to start talking to your children is when they are between the ages of 9 and 11.
2. Set a good example. Be a good role model. Never drive while drunk.
3. Be factual when discussing the topic of drinking. Don't damage your credibility by using scare tactics, or lecturing. State your position. Provide the facts about drinking and driving.
4. Set firm rules and guidelines. Know where you stand when it comes to drinking.
5. Practice good parenting through family togetherness. This creates an atmosphere of open communication, trust, and respect.

6. Get to know your child's friends and extended family members. Discuss the powerful influences of peer pressure. Encourage positive friendships.
7. Get help promptly if you know your child has a drinking problem.

Ohlms then pointed out how parents are the primary role models for their children. He said, "Don't turn alcohol into something totally evil. It makes it more attractive."

The video showed several situations with alcohol and a child, and how to handle them. The viewer was shown how to turn tough questions from children into a learning process. One message was that it is important to use a tough love approach where drinking is concerned.

A survey was quoted showing parents influence young people on the decision of whether or not to drink 60% of the time, whereas friends influence them only 17% of the time. Children look to their parents as their primary role models.

The *Family Talk* campaign endorsed drinking in our society as not being a problem as long as one is responsible. The *responsible model* was put forward. Yet, in today's society, being responsible by itself is not enough of a motivation to handle a drug like alcohol. We need more healthy-choice opportunities in the culture. Alcohol, according to much health research, is the number-one health problem for the society. We need to know how to deal with the problem of alcohol. In its public relations campaign, Anheuser-Busch did not code alcohol as a problem, but instead as a neutral substance. That, of course, raises the issue about how a beer company can produce a public relations campaign like *Family Talk* in the first place.

One might look at the relationship between media messages and drinking among young people in this country. Grube and Wallack (1994) concluded that their findings suggested that attempts to prevent or delay drinking among young people should give attention to alcohol *advertising*. Lipman (1991) showed that a survey conducted by an alcohol industry group found that 73% of the general public agreed that alcohol advertising is a major contributor to underage drinking.

This chapter set out to examine the ideology of the public service campaign *Family Talk* in the light of the health model presented from researchers in alcohol abuse prevention. The objective was to deconstruct a media text in relationship to the political, economic, and, in this case, health environment in the culture. What we found first was that alcohol in itself is not coded as a problem. Second, the model of abuse prevention presented is responsible drinking. This is not the current model used in health care (the risk reduction lifestyle model is the model presently put forth).

Thus, one can see that a community relations campaign is not just simply servicing the community. The text also involves an ideology and a value system that support one group over another—the brewery industry over the health care community—and, therefore, one ideology over another.

Family Talk was off target for two reasons. First, the prevention model is not appropriate for today's society, where there are so many problems connected with alcohol. Second, it did not address alcohol advertising, which is so prevalent in our society and whose messages are not only in ads but in other forms of promotion.

A more appropriate approach to address alcohol might be teaching children media literacy, so that they can analyze and evaluate the persuasive appeals in public relations materials about alcohol. Garrett, Freay, Wildasin, and Hobbs (1995) defined media literacy as the ability to analyze, augment, and influence the active reading or viewing of media so that one can become an effective citizen.

REFERENCES

Altman, K. E. (1990). Consuming ideology: The better homes in America campaign. *Critical Studies in Mass Communication, 7*, 286–307.

Carey, J. W. (1975). A cultural approach to communication. *Communication, 2*, 1–22.

Coffin, J. G. (1994). Credit, consumption, and images of women's desires: Selling the sewing machine in late nineteenth-century France. *French Historical Studies, 18*(3), 749–783.

Daugherty, R., & O'Bryan, T. (1987). *Blueprints for change: Exploring the models for prevention of alcohol and drug problems*. Lexington, KY: Prevention Research Institute.

Finn, A., & Strickland, D. (1982). A content analysis of beverage alcohol advertising. *Journal of Studies in Alcohol, 43*, 964–989.

Flora, J. (1993, May) . *Where is health communication research going?* Paper presented at annual meeting of International Communication Association in Washington, DC.

Garrett, S. D., Freay, J., Wildasin, M., & Hobbs, R. (1995). *Messages and meaning: A guide to understanding media*. Newark, DE: International Reading Association.

Grube, J., & Wallack, L. (1994). Television beer advertising and drinking knowledge, relief, and intentions among school children. *American Journal of Public Health, 84*(2), 254–258.

Kellner, D. (1995). No respect disciplinary and media studies: Media communications vs. Cultural studies. *Communication Theory, 5*(2), 162–178.

Lipman, J. (1991, Aug. 21). Sobering view: Alcohol firms put off public. *Wall Street Journal*, p. B1.

Madden, P., & Grube, J. W. (1994). The frequency and nature of alcohol and tobacco advertising in televised sports, 1990 through 1992. *American Journal of Public Health, 84*(2), 297–299.

Mosher, J. (1994). Alcohol advertising and public health: An urgent call for action. *American Journal of Public Health, 84*(2), 180–181.

Porter, W. M. (1992). The environment of the oil company: A semiotic analysis of Chevron's 'people do' commercials. In E. L. Toth & R. L. Heath (Eds.), *Rhetorical and critical approaches to public relations* (pp. 279–300). Hillsdale, NJ: Lawrence Erlbaum Associates.

Toth, E. L., & Heath, R. L. (1992). *Rhetorical and critical approaches to public relations*. Hillsdale, NJ: Lawrence Erlbaum Associates.

Wilcox, D., Ault, P., & Agee, W. (1995). *Public relations strategies and tactics*. New York: HarperCollins.

CHAPTER EIGHT

The Language of Mental Illness

This chapter looks at the public relations text from the perspective of hermeneutics. Hermeneutic experience, which is the paradigm of our experience of the world, takes place in language and consists in conversation with a text (Weinsheimer, 1985). Here, we deconstruct a six-panel brochure that must be both written and understood within a historical and cultural context that the reader and the writer share through a common system of language.

At one time or another, most public relations writers use the controlled media form of a brochure as a matter of course in their job. What we'd like to see here is a way to understand the brochure less from a communication as transmission point of view. Therefore, this chapter takes a theoretically different perspective. As Hall (1975) did, we approach the public relations text as a structure of meanings rather than as a channel for the sending and receiving of information.

A theory is a way to look at something and ought to enlighten a problem. In the social sciences and natural sciences, theory is commonly used as the basis for prediction and control, yet the essence of all theory is to offer interpretation.

Hermeneutics helps us see that language is a way of understanding being. Our language makes possible a common experience precisely because we seek to use language that is already part of that experience.

In public relations, some scholars point to a real lack of theories. Botan (1989) said that, with few exceptions, public relations has not systematically addressed the development of theory or the relationship of practice to research and theory building.

Dance (1982) asserted that the bulk of Anglo-American communication theory is primarily influenced by positivism. If, in the natural sciences, it has so far been impossible to find any single theory that can explain "everything," then surely we are not likely to find one in the social sciences (Halloran, 1983). There certainly is the need for a variety of ways to talk about and do research in the area of public relations.

A problem with much public relations theory building is that the research seems to come from administrative studies, which tend to be more normative. What seems lacking is a more critical or historical kind of theory building rather than a behavioral kind of theory building. There are, however, some important examples to consider in public relations theory building.

It is possible to distinguish several different theories or perspectives emerging in public relations. First is general systems theory as applied to public relations. Broom (1986) described the public relations concern with goal setting and program planning as part of the general systems model. Long and Hazelton (1987) described general systems theory as a meta-theoretical approach for organizing public relations phenomena. Grunig and Grunig (1986) considered systems theory as the most important paradigm for public relations.

A second approach to public relations is critical theory, specifically feminist theory, as discussed by Rankow (1989). The feminization of public relations should be recognizable as nothing less than a gender crisis for the whole field, triggered by the entrance of substantial numbers of women, but fed by a long-standing conflict over ideologies of power and control.

A third approach is the rhetorical theory of Kenneth Burke applied to public relations. According to Rybacki and Rybacki (1987), Burke's theory of dramatism should be the paradigm of choice of public relations, because public relations departments and agencies are self-consciously in the business of making dramas using the symbol system of language.

A fourth theory, introduced by Kruckeberg and Starck (1988), takes a symbolic interactionist approach to public relations. Rather than advocacy for an organization or a client, the professional in public relations should be responsible for relationships among and between groups.

And finally, borrowing from the work of Berger and Luckman, White (1987) looked at public relations as the social construction of reality. He argued that public relations contributes to the social construction of reality by putting forward information for negotiation regarding its meaning and by contributing to the process of negotiation itself.

The approach to public relations presented in this chapter is more closely aligned with the critical, historical tradition. One might characterize the present discussion as a phenomenological approach to deconstruction.

Because public relations professionals spend so much time writing, it is important to discuss how we understand through language. Language is not simply something one uses to target an audience, but is also used as the way to understand and be understood in a particular culture and time.

In the field of theology (and the field of law to some extent), the history of hermeneutics has traditionally centered on textual interpretation. The hermeneutical objective is to see the text as an experience. In reading the words, the reader understands (experiences) its meaning for himself/herself today. Biblical scholars like Bultman have sought to demythologize the Bible, which simply means to get rid of the myths and baggage connected with the word and let the word speak to the reader as *kerygma* (challenge). Notice that in biblical hermeneutics the word is not simply a means to get a message across, but is also the experience. The biblical writer chose certain words that were part of a time and culture. As someone today reads that word, not only must he/she understand the time and culture of the wording, but that contextualizing becomes the way to understand the word as it speaks today. From its roots in theology one can see that hermeneutics shows us that words are ways of relating and of experience; they are not simply instruments or signs to get a message across to the reader. The reader and the writer are historical beings situated in a time and culture.

Translation from one language to another makes us conscious of the clash of our own world of understanding and that in which the work is operating. In biblical study, one is faced with the problem of understanding the word as a translation. Hermeneutics is concerned with interpretation as the way to understand the text in the present culture.

Hermeneutics as a way of understanding forces us to face questions of ontology and epistemology. Who are we as human beings? We exist as beings open to experience, as beings in process, as becoming. How do we come to know? We *understand* by being open to the language given in our culture. We understand ourselves and our world through language. We experience our world through the language of our world.

There are two schools of hermeneutics. First, the Schleiermacher and Dilthey approach, which is called the "objectification of texts." In the eighteenth century, Schleiermacher held that our understanding of a text takes place in a "hermeneutical circle." We understand a word in a sentence by seeing it in reference to the whole sentence. By dialectical interaction between the whole and the part, each gives the other meaning; understanding is circular. The goal of hermeneutics is the reconstruction of the mental experience of the text's author. Schleiermacher moved away from a language-centered hermeneutics to one centered on the individuality of the author.

Dilthey did not want the method of natural science applied to the study of the person, but did hold that concrete experience and not speculation must be the source for understanding. His view was how do we get in touch with lived experience except through what is "objectively valid" (Palmer, 1969).

Under Dilthey's purview, art is the preeminent expression of lived experience, more than ideas or action because art points to life itself. Therefore, art is the most reliable, enduring, and fruitful object of all human studies. Of all artworks, those in language have perhaps the greatest power to disclose the inner life of humans. For Dilthey, hermeneutics was not merely text interpretation but how life discloses and expresses itself in words (Palmer, 1969). The artwork, especially in language, has a fixed, enduring, objective status; thus, human studies could envision the possibility of objectively valid knowledge, because the object was relatively unchanging in itself. To understand art is to understand humans in history. For Dilthey, hermeneutics was the study of humans through objectification of art, especially as expressed in language.

The second major school of hermeneutics began with Heidegger, who saw hermeneutics from a wider perspective than did Dilthey and Schleiermacher (i.e., as the understanding of the linguisticality of being; Palmer, 1969). Heidegger remarked how erroneous to think that humans invent language any more than they invent understanding, time, or being itself: "How could man ever have invented the power which pervades him, which alone enables him to be as a man?" (Palmer, 1969, p. 154). The very essence of language has the hermeneutical function of bringing a thing to show itself.

Gadamer, a student of Heidegger, took a similar position about hermeneutics and language. Words are not something that belong to the person, but instead to the situation. They are not a sign. The devising of words to describe experience is no random act, but instead is a conforming to the demands of the experience.

Public relations writing also both conforms to the experience and arises from the experience. The words are not simply tools to get a message out to others.

Gadamer said that form cannot be separated from content, but when we think of language in instrumental terms, we automatically do so. Experience is not so much something that comes prior to language, but rather experience itself occurs in and through language (Palmer, 1969).

Gadamer called hermeneutics understanding through dialogue. We "converse" in and through language. We live and understand ourselves and our experience through language. In understanding a text, as in political diplomacy or collective bargaining, transmission of a concept is not the goal. The criterion of textual understanding is not recovery of the author's meaning, but discovery of a common meaning, one that is shared by the interpreter (Weinsheimer, 1985).

Understanding is always an historical, dialectical, linguistic event—in the sciences and in the humanities. For Gadamer, according to Palmer (1969), hermeneutics was the ontology and phenomenology of understanding.

It is important to realize that, for Gadamer, language was *the* way of being and knowing. Truth is historically situated through language. The keys to understanding are not manipulation and control, but instead participation and openness; not knowledge, but instead experience (Palmer, 1969).

One does not invent and manipulate language to suit oneself; you participate in language and allow a situation to come to stand in language (Palmer, 1969). Language has no independent life apart from the world that comes to language within it. Deetz (1973) noted that Gadamer suggested that words do not belong to people, but instead to the situation.

Palmer (1969) proposed 30 theses at the end of his book on hermeneutics. This is thesis #6: "The Hermeneutical Experience is Objective" (p. 243). What Palmer meant is that we do not use our world, history, or language; we participate in them. Language is not a tool one uses, but instead is the way being can come to appear. When we wish to convey the being of a situation, we do not devise language to fit it so much as to find the language demanded by the situation.

From this hermeneutical perspective, we would now like to look at the text that the public relations practitioner creates. There are several assumptions from hermeneutics in pursuing such a course.

First, we do not control our audience with our words. Rather, our words are the experience for both ourselves as author and for the reader, because we have to make the experience understandable or objectified.

Second, words assume a dialogical process for both the author and the reader. They become the third corner of the hermeneutical triangle. We don't just dialogue through words; we dialogue "with" words. The hermeneutical triangle's three corners are: the author, the reader, and the word.

Third, the public relations text must be understood historically. Its truth lies in the encounter with negativity (Palmer, 1969). The emphasis again is dialogue *with* words. Truth is not conceived as correspondence of statements to "fact," but rather as the dynamic emergence of being into the light of manifestness. The experience comes as "language event." Truth is not conceptual—it happens in and through understanding primarily in language. According to Gadamer, it is historical life, not logical consistency, that is the final arbiter and ground of truth (Weinsheimer, 1985). Whatever we read is not information but language to be interpreted and thus experienced in some way.

Fourth, understanding has no method, according to Gadamer. It is not a procedure that one can choose to apply or not, or for which there are either better or worse alternatives. One does not decide to understand circularly. There is no other way. Hermeneutics is not a method applied to understanding, then, but *understanding itself* (Weinsheimer, 1985).

Finally, we project our prejudices on the text. Prejudices are cultural. We do not choose our prejudices, because we discover them in ourselves as things that exist prior to our conscious choice. Yet, this priority to consciousness does not make them subjective either, because prejudices derive not from a private subconscious but from a communal tradition.

The public relations text we deconstruct here is a six-panel brochure from the American Mental Health Fund, founded in 1983 by Jack and Jo Ann Hinkley, parents of John Hinkley.[1]

The brochure uses three phrases that form the substance of its text. First, language about mental illness is one of "silence." We don't talk about it. Second, there is presently a "cry for help." Third, people who suffer from this illness and their families want a "cure." There is a search for a cure going on right now. Friends are needed to help fund the search for a cure.

The image of the young girl in Fig. 8.1 is on the front panel, accompanied by the words "When the mentally ill cry out for help what they usually say is … nothing at all." The last three words appear in the first inside panel. Note that the girl embodies an unwillingness to talk or discuss what is bothering her, which in this case we are supposed to read as mental illness.

The text discusses how silence has been the way to treat the illness. In the past we would lock victims of mental illness in asylums and dark cellars. But there is still silence today, because only one of every five victims of the disease seeks help.

The rest of the brochure highlights the organization called the American Mental Health Fund that has helped tens of thousands of families by providing them with information about mental illness and a place to turn to for help. But now, in addition to public information campaigns, they would like to use the money they receive to seek cures for the illness.

The conclusion challenges the reader to end America's terrible silence. Let the American Mental Health Fund become the advo-

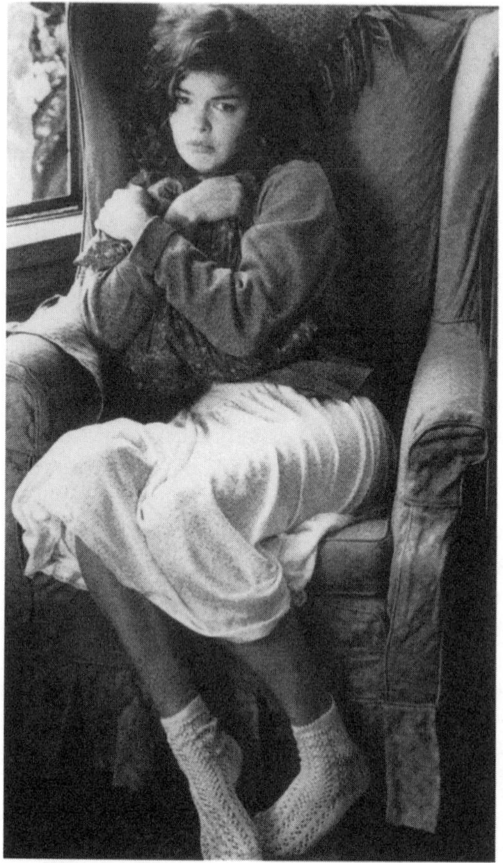

FIG. 8.1 Girl on the front cover of a brochure from the American Mental Health Fund.

cate for research and programs for the mentally ill. The reader is asked to send a tax-deductible gift today.

The interpretation of the text of the brochure first of all assumes the format of a persuasive brochure. The writer wants to move the reader to action. The language creates the current understanding of mental illness. The writer has to dialogue with the language and the reader. The author must write in the historical moment of his/her culture and its prejudices.

We are using language, and language is using us. We are shaped by language. The writer does not stand outside of culture as one who decides to use certain words. He/she uses the words that speak his/her culture and history.

Words are self-critical, and open-ended. We are changed by them. All language is not simply informational or rhetorical, but *dialogical*. We *become* a part of our culture by the words we use in that culture.

The reader experiences the language in its historical context. The history of treating this illness has been meager. Today we *can* change that. The way the author writes about the illness *is* the experience for the reader.

The words tell the reader the experience of mental illness can be understood as "illness," and like any illness can be cured. Mental illness was not always seen as it "is" today (i.e., curable). We experience the illness in our words about it. The key words describing mental illness are *silence, help*, and *cure*.

As hermeneutics points out, the words are not just vehicles to get the message across, but also form the experience of the writer as he/she seeks to historicize the illness for both himself/herself *and* the reader. Together, they dialogue in the words used. As the reader, you ask yourself: Why has mental illness been shrouded in silence? Is there a cure? How does this affect me? The language of the brochure stimulates this kind of dialogue. At the same time, the words themselves are open-ended, which means they challenge the reader to go beyond, to think, to speculate, to interpret *for the present moment as he/she reads* and finds that the words may raise more questions than give answers.

History enables us to experience mental illness as curable. History is experienced or interpreted in the language we use. One hundred years ago, we couldn't talk or write about mental illness in this way, nor could we 50 years ago, perhaps not even 25 years ago. If we did, we would not be in touch with our experience. Language creates the experience at a historical moment. If we want to be "understood," we speak and write in words that create experience for the listener or reader, but at the same time we must write in and out of the culture of which we are part. As public relations writers, we do not stand above or beyond that context.

The text is an unfinished process; one that is continually completed in the history of its being understood (Weinsheimer, 1985). "The fact that the human word is not one but many; the fact that the object of thought is not wholly realized in any one of its conceptions, impels it constantly forward toward further words and concepts, and gives it an essentially unlimited freedom to produce new ones" (p. 237).

Writing is not getting a message across, but instead creating an experience through language that is understood by the reader as an entity in its own right. As writers, we don't just choose this word rather than that—we get in touch with the experience of the words we use. Our readers do the same. We use the language of our culture and thus we—the writer, reader, and language—create our own culture.

Hermeneutics helps us understand the role of language for experience. The language of the world of mental illness 25 or 50 years ago did not allow discussion of the kind we share today. Our experience of the illness is found in the language we use, and that language helps us understand/experience the persons involved. Such is the view of hermeneutics, a phenomenological approach to language and understanding in which language is seen not as a derivative (a tool) but as a *way of being* in the world.

Like some of the more critical, historical approaches presented at the beginning of this chapter, hermeneutics offers much as a theoretical source for *understanding* public relations and placing public relations in a less mechanist or positivist approach. In that effort, a theory like hermeneutics increases our understanding of the field.

In this chapter, a theory called hermeneutics was used to help deconstruct public relations writing. What we have shown is a way to understand public relations from a phenomenological perspective. We are just scratching the surface here, but it certainly is a path that offers much insight for both the writer and the reader of public relations material.

Here are some implications for the public relations writer:

- Words are not tools but instead are the source of the experience for the writer and reader.
- As writers, we need to understand the language that creates our world.

- Language is part of the dialective that, like the reader and the author, needs to be seen as in process and therefore as a living entity.
- Words need to be taken in context for understanding. We understand the whole through its parts—we understand the parts in relation to the whole.
- As writers, we need to listen to words and be open to what they call us to do or become.
- As readers, we need to listen to words and be open to what they call us to do or become.

REFERENCES

Botan, C. (1989, May). *Public relations as applied to social science: The role of theory development*. Paper presented at the annual meeting of the International Communication Association, San Francisco.

Broom, G. M. (1986, May). *Public relations roles and systems theory: Functional and historicist causal models*. Paper presented at the annual meeting of the International Communication Association, Chicago.

Dance, F. E. (1982). *Human communication theory*. New York: Harper & Row.

Deetz, S. (1973). Words without things: Toward a social phenomenology of language. *Quarterly Journal of Speech, 59*, 40–51.

Grunig, J. E., & Grunig, L. S. (1986, May). *Application of open systems theory to public relations: Review of open systems theory*. Paper presented at the annual meeting of the International Communication Association, Chicago.

Hall, S. (1975). Introduction. In A. C. Smith et al., *Paper voices* (pp. 11–24). Washington, DC: Rowan and Littlefield.

Halloran, J. D. (1983). A case for critical eclecticism. *Journal of Communication, 33*(3), 270–301.

Kruckeberg, D., & Starck, K. (1988). *Public Relations and community: A reconstructed theory* . New York: Praeger.

Long, L. W., & Hazelton, V., Jr. (1987). Public relations: A theoretical and practical response. *Public Relations Review, 13*(2), 3–13.

Palmer, R. E. (1969). *Hermeneutics*. Evanston, IL: Northwestern University Press.

Rankow, L. F. (1989, May). *From the feminization of public relations to the promise of feminism*. Paper presented at the annual meeting of the International Communication Association, San Francisco.

Rybacki, K., & Rybacki, D., (1987, November). *Public rhetoric and public relations*. Paper presented at the annual meeting of the Speech Communication Association, Boston.

Weinsheimer, J. (1985). *Gadamer's hermeneutics: A reading of truth and method*. New Haven, CT: Yale University Press.

White, J. (1987, August). *Public relations in the social construction of reality: Theoretical and practical implications of Berger and Luckmann's view of social construction of reality*. Paper presented at the annual meeting of the Association for Education in Journalism and Mass Communication, San Antonio.

ENDNOTE

[1]John Hinkley attempted to assassinate President Ronald Reagan in 1981. He was found not guilty by reason of insanity, and is currently incarcerated in a Washington, DC, psychiatric hospital.

CHAPTER NINE

The Ideology of an AIDS Prevention Campaign

There is a tradition in the both the study and the practice of public relations to see the field as a social science. For example, Botan and Hazelton (1989) noted that public relations may be studied as an applied social science, and the same theoretical and research tools of other social sciences may be useful in studying public relations. This chapter argues that we can also study public relations from a humanities perspective, using cultural studies as a critical theory to understand public relations.

The feminist research area in public relations has used the critical approach (Creedon, 1991). Moffitt (1994) did a critical and cultural analysis as she looked at the concept of image in public relations.

Potter, Cooper, and Dupagne (1994) asserted that the study of mass media has three paradigms—social science, interpretive, and critical—but by far the largest body of literature is from the social science view. The research paradigm for public relations has also been mainly from the social science model, whereas what the field needs is more research based on critical theory. Such thinking, however, still contradicts the major stream of scholarship in the field. For one to propose a critical theory of public relations practice seems to mean rowing against the tide. Yet, such bold action seems more necessary at this time than ever, because mainstream media are becoming more dependent on information from public relations sources. For example, most TV stations now routinely use video news releases from public relations sources whereas a few years ago only about half did so.

Kuhn (1970) maintained that the predominant paradigm in a field has become so because people have not looked at the issue from other perspectives. He wrote:

> Normal science, which is cumulative, owes its success to the ability of scientists regularly to select problems that can be solved with conceptual and instrumental techniques close to those already in existence. The person who is striving to solve a problem defined by existing knowledge and technique is not just looking around. He knows what he wants to achieve, and he designs his instruments and directs his thoughts accordingly. (p. 96)

New ways of thinking about the field are particularly relevant to the area of public relations which, according to Grunig (1993), has been building its own body of theory and research using mostly a social science model.

The task of the public relations professional is to plan and actualize communication with a significant public about a product or service important to both the organization and its public. Edward Bernays (1988), the father of modern public relations practice, defined public relations as that particular field of action that advises a client or an employer on the attitude or action to take to win over the publics on whom the employer depends. Such a definition implies that the public needs an initial openness to the client's cause or issue.

The practice of public relations dates back to the turn of the twentieth century, when it became a recognized field of professional endeavor. Journalists like Ivy Lee became consultants for clients who needed favorable press. Because, as former journalists, they knew the newspaper business, their job was often to write positive news stories about their clients and get the stories placed in local or national newspapers. The same thing happens today, only the medium has changed; now a public relations professional may also use more interactive electronic media, like the Internet. The role of the public relations professional who is often both consultant and writer is to get the word out about a company and thus create a favorable environment in which that organization can do its business.

Most organizations today have an internal public relations staff that performs the day-to-day role of getting the word out about the organization's service or product. Whether in the corporate sector, human services, the arts, or even the government, no organization can survive today without sound public relations.

The public relations practitioner must code his/her written and spoken message in the cultural values of the day, and in doing so the campaign often embodies an ideology that supports the status quo. The status quo may mean that certain groups in the society are alienated, because they do not appear "normal" nor behave in what the majority defines as "normal."

The objective of this chapter is to deconstruct a government-sponsored public relations health campaign, and argue that in the text a significant public has been ignored in order to get the message acceptable to the general public. The ignored segment, the homosexual audience, is not just a part of the general public but has been defined as a specific public or target audience for the campaign by many health professionals.

Bawer (1993) noted that the gay person has no place in society today, because of general ignorance about homosexuality in our culture. People fear what they do not know. That fear generates a sense of difference, but always through the symbol of word and image.

The Centers for Disease Control (CDC) have been the major national player in mounting a campaign about AIDS prevention. The CDC, under the Department of Health and Human Services (HHS), is the principal federal agency responsible for preventing AIDS through education. It may simply be ignorance in our society that has forced the CDC to downplay the image of the homosexual in its campaign for AIDS prevention and awareness. It is not the intention here to question motivation, but instead to examine outcomes (i.e., the public relations text). We undertake a critical textual analysis of a video campaign produced by the CDC to address AIDS in this country.

Public service announcements (PSAs) are more effective when they provide information about topics on which people generally agree (O'Keefe & Reid, 1990). It could be that because there is so much ignorance and controversy concerning the homosexual lifestyle, the CDC's video campaign does not make any reference to gay America. We see the CDC's choice through their promotional material, especially in their video PSAs, which, because they wind up on the major networks, are produced for the largest number of consumers.

Seidman (1988) argued that AIDS is not a gay disease. The only statement that can be endorsed unequivocally is that specific homosexual acts are high risk. AIDS affects the homosexual community because they are at risk. There is a need to disseminate credible information about homosexuality in order to facilitate behavior that reduces people's risk of contracting AIDS. Seidman noted, "AIDS requires credible empirical knowledge of homosexuality. This will stimulate and legitimate research on homosexuals, much of which will challenge stereotypes" (p. 203).

AIDS is a serious health issue for the world. An estimated 1 million to 1.5 million Americans are infected with the Human Immunodeficiency Virus (HIV), the virus that causes AIDS. In the early 1990s, it was estimated that one in every 100 adult males and one in every 800 adult females was infected with HIV (AIDS Action Committee, 1992).

The demographics of the victim list of this disease included both homosexuals and heterosexuals. In New England in the 1990s, homosexual men made up the largest group of new cases at 48% (New AIDS Definition, 1993). On the international scene, however, 75% of all cases were transmitted through heterosexual sex (AIDS Action Committee, 1992), but homosexual and bisexual men were the most affected group (Pollak, 1992). The 1993 Massachusetts Surveillance Statistics reported that 56% of U.S. AIDS cases at that time were homosexual or bisexual males (1993). One conference on AIDS prevention recommended a group-specific approach as essential if one defined prevention no longer exclusively as information dissemination, but instead in terms of interactive and/or ritualized learning of new behaviors (Pollak, 1992).

AIDS is also a political concern at the federal, state, and local levels. The Senate and Congress have responded primarily through support in funding. Local town leaders and school boards want to avoid bringing it up to schools, yet junior high and high school students are at high risk for contracting the disease. In the 1990s, the number of reported AIDS cases among 13- to 21-year-olds doubled every 14 months (Stephenson & Walsh-Childers, 1993). There is a paradox in our country: We need to understand and do something about the relationship between sexual behavior and the risk of AIDS; yet we don't want our schools to address the topic of sex. The media nonetheless continue to use sex as the magic vehicle to sell almost everything.

The government is faced with the problem of dealing with reaching several conflicting goals. The most important goal is trying to prevent the AIDS virus from spreading. The government must do this while trying not to offend the majority of the public's moral views on sex. Finally, the government is faced with the task of keeping people safe who are either already infected or at high risk of contracting AIDS.

AIDS is a highly visible politicized disease in the United States, with a 1991 death total of 45,000, less then one tenth the number of deaths from cancer and equal in number to those killed in traffic accidents. Two-thirds of new cases are linked to homosexuals and drug abusers. Among heterosexuals, the disease has spread mainly within the Hispanic and African American communities. The National Commission on Acquired Immune Deficiency Syndrome accused the senior (George H.) Bush administration of ignoring its recommendation for major financial support for AIDS. Spending had increased only 4% in 1992. Proposals to increase funding, particularly for patient care, were not adopted by that Bush administration. It seems that former President George H. Bush did not want to be known as the leader of the war on AIDS, which impression, some have argued, would have alienated his conservative base of support (Greenberg, 1992).

The media also has an agenda on the issue of AIDS. Notice the difficulty HBO had in late 1993 in producing their made-for-TV film *The Band Played On*, based on the award-winning history of the origins of the AIDS epidemic—and its resulting politicization—by journalist Randy Shilts, who eventually succumbed to the disease. Richard Gere, one of the stars of the HBO film, had said that the producers needed to get a big-name actor in order to make the film acceptable to conservative audiences. One year later, however, in 1994, the film *Philadelphia* was celebrated as one that addressed both AIDS and the gay lifestyle with honesty and dignity. *Philadelphia* earned both box office success and an

Academy Award for its star, Tom Hanks (who arguably became a big-name actor because of this film).

The CDC remain the principal U.S. player responsible for preventing AIDS, through information and education. The CDC's AIDS activities include education programs aimed at curtailing the epidemic's spread and epidemiology and surveillance programs. Through these activities, the CDC track the spread of AIDS and can better target AIDS education efforts. Between fiscal years 1984 and 1988, the CDC's total AIDS budget grew more than 100% each year on average, from $14 million to over $300 million. (General Accounting Office, 1988).

The CDC, however, face many problems. One of their main difficulties seems to be that the government has a strong political hold on the agency (Susser, 1993). A majority of health experts consider the most effective way of controlling a disease like AIDS is through prevention, not through treatment of victims. Nonetheless, conservative politicians who find controversy in "safe sex" education consider AIDS research politically neutral. Thus, drug development funding outpaces funding for prevention, leaving people who do not yet have the disease at greater risk for contracting it (Thompson, 1990).

The CDC public relations campaign to be examined here is called "America Responds to AIDS." The CDC produced a series of video and audio PSAs as part of the campaign. More than $105 million has gone toward a national AIDS information campaign, which included a toll-free hotline as well as paid advertisements (Booth, 1988).

Freimuth, Hammond, Edgar, & Monahan (1990) found that the PSAs did not target specific groups, but instead were often made for the general public. They do not acknowledge the differences among such segments as homosexuals, bisexuals, women, adolescent heterosexuals, IV drug users, and minority groups (Freimuth, 1992). Government media campaigns, trying to address "everybody" at the same time, are unlikely to be able to respond to the diversity of need (Markova & Power, 1992).

Every public service campaign supports a political agenda and, at the same time, espouses a value system. Some of the criteria for PSAs are that they must be sufficiently national in scope and appeal to a general, national audience. They must also deal affirmatively with a cause, and not attack others. Paletz, Pearson, and Willis (1977) argued that, primarily through PSAs, a particular set of political attitudes has been conveyed to the American public. Paletz et al. stressed the importance of conveying a message aimed at different audiences. Although a PSA may look like it is serving the public good, the choice of visuals and language in the text indicates that great care has been taken not to alienate audience members by a less-than-conservative way of thinking.

Perhaps one cannot expect more from television. Television in this country is not a force for change as much as it is a force for stability, which Gerbner, Gross, Morgan, and Signorielli (1986) called the homogenization effect of television mainstreaming (p. 31). Mainstreaming thus made television the true twentieth-century melting pot of the American people, according to Littlejohn (1992).

TV advertising, and one might make a case for a public service announcement as well, also approaches its target audience through supporting a middle-of-the-road value system or cultural norm underlying the product or service it promotes: not too conservative and not too liberal, in order not to distance the audience (Wermick, 1991). The programming choices of television networks need to embody a similar content in order to keep advertisers happy. For example, when the CDC began its "America Responds to AIDS" campaign between December 1987 and February 1988, nearly 90% of all network-aired AIDS public service announcements were shown during non-prime-time viewing hours, with 59% being shown between 11 p.m. and 7 a.m. (General Accounting Office, 1988).

This chapter is concerned with the deconstruction of the text produced by the public relations professional. Thus, one might also say the focus of this research is the decoding of a cultural artifact.

With words in speech and writing, we describe same-sex and other-sex relations. Through words, we also produce the differences in the culture. We say someone is homosexual, heterosexual, or bisexual and that saying is a way of being in the culture. Without saying the word, there is no being or production of difference. Suppression of same-sex sexuality happens by absence of discourse. If we don't say it or show it, then it has no value in the culture.

Sedgwick (1993), who does research on sexuality from a cultural studies perspective, wrote, "A T-shirt that ACT UP sells in New York bearing the text 'I am out, therefore I am,' is meant to do for the wearer, not the constative work of reporting that s/he is out, but the performative work of coming out in the first place" (p. 246).

Cultural studies is a way to look at how the culture codes its values and ideology, particularly through products that have large cultural acceptance and have become almost second nature to the consumer, like the jingles of TV advertising. Johnson (1987) proposed three ways to approach cultural studies as a critical theory: from a production-based model, from the view of the text, and from studies of lived cultures. Here is the approach of the *text*. When viewing the text, however, we are concerned with the political and economic environment in which the text takes on its meaning. We make sense of the words and images of the text in terms of the context in which it appears and which it proximately and ultimately defines.

Cultural studies has been concerned with looking at media as a way to understand the culture. Looking at public relations material might be another way of understanding the culture. The premise of the cultural studies approach is a critical view of an individual media product in terms of its political and economic context (Harms & Kellner, 1991). A critical view of advertising, for example, ought to look at the kind of social order advertising creates: where the powerful and the powerless are produced in the text. The ultimate criticism of advertising is not that advertising creates false needs, but that it molds real needs and passions into distorted social relationships (Harms & Kellner, 1991).

Sexuality has often been coded in media products for certain cultural goals. Although gender roles (for both men and women) seem to be somewhat less restricted today, use of gender representations in advertising continues to serve not the growth of gender definitions, but rather the continuance of the economic system (Kervin, 1990). In her cultural studies look at the public relations of the Better Homes campaign from the 1920s, Altman showed how women were coded as homemakers and men as homebuilders (1990). The cultural product called an ad makes sense only in terms of that culture, and thus was selling more than a product—it was selling a way to be and a way to behave.

To deconstruct cultural artifacts like PSAs is to look at the text as a product of ideology. Agger (1992) argued that cultural studies should take a Marxist view so we might see that culture is at once a normative and material practice. Although culture transmits values, the encoding of these values is often subtle, even contradicting the express intent of particular cultural transmissions. For example, public service announcements on the theme of talking to your kids about alcohol even before their teenage years, as suggested in an ad in *Newsweek*, normalizes alcohol in a culture and thus alcohol is an accepted and unproblematic way of dealing with the world.

Carey (1989) defended the importance and centrality of cultural studies because, he said, "Ideology and power are central to social life. They are less than the whole cloth, however. After all, ideology plays a larger role in modern life because coercion plays a much smaller role. Ideological state apparatuses have significantly displaced repressive state apparatuses" (p. 108).

One approach to cultural analysis is to look at the semiotics of the text. A method to do so was presented in the work of Lanigan (1988), who proposed three steps: description, reduction, and interpretation. The method used here is similar; that is, to describe and offer an interpretation of the video PSAs' text.

In general, media producers like public relations professionals are not necessarily aware of the ideology they promote in their products. After all, what they intend to do is to get a message that they conceptualize as important out to a specific public.

We might state the research problem in the following way: In order not to promote the gay lifestyle, the CDC's "America Responds to AIDS" video PSA campaign does not mention the risk of AIDS for the homosexual viewer. Thus, the CDC codes the illness as not affecting the group most at risk.

The CDC's video PSAs are the media vehicles that are seen by most members of the American public. The posters, pamphlets, and so on are more apt to be seen by a smaller number of people (e.g., those who ride public transportation or those who go into doctors' offices).

What follows is an examination of four PSAs produced by the CDC and subsequently offered in their catalog (1993). The videos were available free of charge to anyone interested. Following each script is a commentary on that video.

PSA #1: AMERICA (60 SECONDS)

The scene opens with a porch of white house. The sun is shining. A bike and red chair along with a blowing American flag attached to the side of the house can be seen.

Announcer: This year more then 40,000 Americans are expected to become infected with HIV. Fortunately many people have found a way to respond.

The second scene is of a laundromat in which a group of young people are talking. One woman is attaching an HIV poster to the window of the store.

Young Man: I got a friend that's got AIDS.
Young Woman: What? They're shooting up?
Other Woman: You think that's the only way people get AIDS?

The next scene is of a middle-aged black man leaning in a chair against a white wall of a brick building. He is sitting on the sidewalk in a busy city. He is reading something.

Announcer: They're educating themselves.
Black Man: If someone is infected with HIV without a blood test ...

A group of lawyers, some young, are sitting around a conference table in their expensive office. Shelves are filled with law books.

A robed black minister stands outside a white country church after the Sunday morning service. He greets people as they leave on this sunny day.

Announcer: They are a congregation and friends.
Black Man: Enlightening sermon.

Minister: I'm glad you think so.

Black Lady: We need to talk to our daughter.

A woman addressing a work crew assembled around her. She is holding papers or notes. They appear to be at a site where a new house is being built.

Announcer: Their community.

Lady: This says that AIDS is growing faster in small towns.

A Chicano father is talking to his son at the kitchen table.

Announcer: Especially their families.

Father to son: You and Nelson (pause). You think you're invincible. No one is.

A shot of a kids playing basketball behind a wire fence. You hear their voices.

Announcer: Education does make a difference.

A woman, Eileen, addresses a group of young women who are all sitting around in what appears to be someone's living room.

Lady to group: My name is Eileen and last year I found out that I have HIV. (At the end, Eileen hugs one of the women.)

Announcer: Each and every one of us must do our part. Find out how you can help prevent AIDS. Call 1-800-342-AIDS.

Commentary: Notice that in words and images of the text AIDS is mentioned as it could affect anyone, from any background, and from any age group. The announcer makes sure we know that education about AIDS is important.

PSA #2: KRISTA (30 SECONDS)

The scene is of a porch of a white house and the sun is shining. A bike, red chair, and a flowing American flag attached to the side of the house appear.
(a voice is heard)

Krista:	The town I live in is so small. Most people don't really think about HIV or AIDS, but my old boyfriend had it and now so do I. You know I found out that AIDS is increasing in small towns. I think it's because people here just don't think it can happen to them.
VISUAL:	Do you want to bet your life on it?
Announcer:	Find out how you can prevent HIV, call 1-800-342-AIDS.
Commentary:	Here we see Krista as just an ordinary, hometown girl who contracted AIDS through sexual contact with her boyfriend in a heterosexual relationship. The emphasis again is on the ordinariness of those who get afflicted by the disease. The ordinary people just happen to be heterosexual, however.

PSA #3: PETER (30 SECONDS)

The scene is of a basketball hoop. You see the fence reflected on the wall.

Peter:	When I was 17 I found out I had HIV. Knowing I could die has been scary, but what's worse is that all my friends are still doing what I did that got me infected and I don't mean drugs. I know that anyone could get HIV but when you're young you think you're invincible. You don't think you'll ever get it.
VISUAL:	Got it!
Announcer:	Find out how you can prevent HIV, call 1-800-342-AIDS
Commentary:	In this PSA, Peter symbolizes young people who could be infected with the disease. Again there is no mention of homosexuality, but the word *drugs* is introduced as not the only way that one can get AIDS. Sexual contact presents a threat as well, but here only heterosexual contact is mentioned.

PSA # 4: FRANKIE (30 SECONDS)

The scene is of a woman's dress hanging by two clothespins on a wash line outside a white house. It's a sunny day and we appear to be in the country.

Frankie:	I always thought that having a man who loved me would keep me safe, until I got HIV. What's bad is that most women still don't protect themselves and I don't want anyone else getting AIDS. Now I do everything I can to teach women that love alone just won't protect them.
VISUAL:	Now a leading cause of death among women. Are you protecting yourself?
Announcer:	Find out how you can prevent HIV, call 1-800-342-AIDS.
Commentary:	The focus here is on women who get AIDS through unprotected heterosexual sex.

All of the PSAs are beautifully photographed and edited. However, one needs to ask why there is so much professionalism but no mention of the homosexual community. Could it be that the CDC do not want to approve the gay lifestyle? Or might it be that the networks that air these PSAs do not want to offend their viewers by promoting homosexuality? Yet, the fact is the homosexual segment of their audience needs to hear that message about preventing AIDS.

It would appear in this text the CDC stay away from the issue of AIDS as it relates to the homosexual lifestyle. The ideology that comes across is that AIDS is not a problem for the homosexual community. In saying that, the CDC forsake the opportunity to educate and inform the public about alternative lifestyles, thereby promoting middle-class, heterosexual values. In order not to promote the gay lifestyle, the CDC's "America Responds to AIDS" video PSA campaign does not mention the risk of AIDS for the homosexual viewer.

In the U.S. mass marketing environment we use a definition of sex to sell products and, in that process, promote a sexual identity. Why can't we, through network TV, educate people about sexually transmitted diseases like AIDS and say that homosexuals are at risk? It could be because we fear promoting the homosexual lifestyle. One has only to think of the debate that raged for months at that time about the controversy in Ellen Degeneres' mid-1990s TV program, "Ellen": Is she lesbian or is she not?

This chapter set out to argue that in order not to promote the gay lifestyle, the CDC's "America Responds to AIDS" video PSA campaign text does not mention the risk of AIDS in the homosexual community. Therefore, the CDC codes the illness as not affecting the group most at risk. The method was to deconstruct the text of the CDC's video public service announcements in the context of current health statistics related to the disease. What the text is saying is not important to the gay viewer.

The analysis of the text was not based solely on the words and images in the videos, but also on the political and economic environment in which television operates in this country. A health care organization like the CDC must buy into the cultural values of the media institutions in order to get free airtime to place its spots. When that happens, the choice of text by the CDC becomes such that it will be acceptable to the gatekeepers at the networks. The message from the CDC therefore becomes one coded in acceptable cultural values and norms. Unfortunately, it becomes the ideology of the status quo.

The challenge from any health care organization has to be to address the health issues as openly and honestly as possible. Sometimes, that happens only when the institution is willing to take a risk. In January 1994, the CDC produced audio PSAs on the theme of using condoms. The campaign generated much controversy because of its explicit language and also the choice of the spokesperson in the spots, a member of the rock group Red Hot Chili Peppers. The CDC could perhaps be criticized for endangering family values, but it might also be commended for deciding to produce the message in cultural values and themes important to the segment of the audience they were trying to reach (i.e., young people). The CDC probably argued for the need to say their message in that way to reach its target audience and thus affirm the cultural values of the young through a rock group representative in order to give the audience a life-saving message.

Public relations work is not simply sending a message to a target audience for the purpose of information or behavior change; it is also an expression of ideology. In that ideology some members of the public may be neglected or slighted in order for the message to receive approval by gatekeepers and acceptance by the general public. The public relations practitioner/communication manager is an individual who uses the cultural values and norms to send a message to important publics or audiences. Cultural values and norms accompany an ideology in that message. When it comes to AIDS, one of the target audiences needs to be the gay viewer, listener, or reader, in spite of any ignorance or prejudice among the general public.

The public relations practitioner promotes cultural norms and values. His/her communication action needs to be open to critical view, to point out the voice that is not being heard in the message, especially in a public relations campaign like that of the CDC. The argument for supporting a cultural studies view of public relations is not simply because it is an alternative perspective, but because, as a critical view of praxis, it is important in a free society.

REFERENCES

Agger, B. (1992). *Cultural studies as critical theory*. Bristol, PA: Falmer.

AIDS Action Committee of Massachusetts, Inc. (1992). *AIDS and HIV fact sheet*. Boston, MA.

Altman, K. (1990). Consuming ideology: The better homes in America campaign. *Critical Studies in Mass Communication, 7*, 286–307.

Bawer, B. (1993). *A place at the table: The gay individual in American society*. Crofton, MO: Poseidon.

Bernays, E. (1988, April). "The meaning of public relations." Lecture given at Bridgewater State College, Bridgewater, MA.

Booth, W. (1988, Oct. 21). Congress passes first AIDS bill. *Science, 21*, p. 367.

Botan, C. H., & Hazelton, V. (Eds.). (1989). *Public relations theory*. Hillsdale, NJ: Lawrence Erlbaum Associates.

Carey, J. (1989). *Communication as culture: Essays on media and society*. Boston: Unwin Hyman.

Centers for Disease Control (CDC) National AIDS Clearinghouse. (1993). *Catalog of HIV and AIDS education and prevention materials*. Rockville, MD: U.S. Department of Health and Human Services.

Creedon, P. J. (1991). Public relations and "women's work": Toward a feminist analysis of public relations roles. *Public Relations Research Annual, 3*, 67–84.

Freimuth, V. S. (1992). Theoretical foundations of AIDS media campaigns. In T. Edgar, M. A. Fitzpatrick, & V. S. Freimuth (Eds.), *AIDS: A communication perspective* (pp. 91–110). Hillsdale, NJ: Lawrence Erlbaum Associates.

Freimuth, V. S., Hammond, S. L., Edgar, T., & Monahan, J. L. (1990). Reaching those at risk: A content-analytic study of AIDS PSAs. *Communication Research, 17*(6), 775–791.

General Accounting Office (1988). *AIDS education: Activities aimed at the general public implemented slowly* (Report to the Honorable Barbara Boxer, House of Representatives). Washington, DC. Author.

Gerbner, G., Gross, L., Morgan, M., & Signorielli, N. (1986). Living with television: The dynamics of the cultivation process. In J. Bryant & D. Zillman (Eds.), *Perspectives on media effects* (pp. 17–40). Hillsdale, NJ: Lawrence Erlbaum Associates.

Greenberg, D. S. (1992). Washington perspective: The new politics of AIDS. *The Lancet, 340*, 105.

Grunig, J. E. (1993). Implications of public relations for other domains of communication. *Journal of Communication, 43*(3), 164–173.

Harms, J., & Kellner, D. (1991). Critical theory and advertising. *Current Perspectives in Social Theory, II*, 410–467.

Johnson, R. (1987). What is cultural studies anyway? *Social Text, 6*(1), 38–80.

Kervin, D. (1990). Advertising masculinity: The representation of males in *Esquire* advertisements. *Journal of Communication Inquiry, 14*(1), 51–70.

Kuhn, T. S. (1970). The structure of scientific revolutions. Chicago: University of Chicago Press.

Lanigan, R. L. (1988). Phenomenology of communication. Pittsburgh: Duquesne University Press.

Littlejohn, S. W. (1992). Theories of human communication (4th ed.). Belmont, C: Wadsworth.

Markova, I., & Power, K. (1992). Audience response to health messages about AIDS. In T. Edgar, M. A. Fitzpatrick, & V. S. Freimuth (Eds.), *AIDS: A communication perspective* (pp. 111–130). Hillsdale, NJ: Lawrence Erlbaum Associates.

Massachusetts Surveillance Statistics. (1993). *AIDS surveillance summary as of July 1, 1993*. SPIN, computer program.

Moffitt, M. A. (1994). A cultural studies perspective toward understanding corporate image: A case study of State Farm Insurance. *Journal of Public Relations Research,* 6(1), 41–63

New AIDS definition adds 48,000 to list. (1993, October 29). *Boston Herald*, p. 4.

O'Keefe, G. J., & Reid, K. (1990). The uses and effects of public service advertising. *Public relations research annual* (Vol. 2). Hillsdale, NJ: Lawrence Erlbaum Associates.

Paletz, D. L., Pearson, R., & Willis, D. (1977). *Politics in public service advertising on television*. New York: Praeger.

Pollak, M. (1992). *Assessing AIDS prevention among male homo- and bisexuals. Assessing AIDS prevention.* (Edited by F. Pacccaud, J. P. Vader, & F. Gutzwiller.) Basel: Birkhauser Verlag.

Potter, J. W., Cooper, R., & Dupagne, M. (1994). The three paradigms of mass media research in mainstream communication journals. *Communication Theory,* 3(4), 317–335.

Sedgwick, E. K. (1993). Axiomatic. In S. During (Ed.), *The cultural studies reader* (pp. 243–268). London: Routledge.

Seidman, S. (1988). Transfiguring sexual identity: AIDS and the contemporary construction of homosexuality. *Social Text, 19/20*, 187–205.

Stephenson, T., & Walsh-Childers, K. (1993, May). *Missing opportunities: Coverage of Magic Johnson and AIDS in magazines popular with teenagers*. Paper presented at the International Communication Association Annual Meeting. Washington, DC.

Susser, M. (1993, May). Emancipate CDC. *American Journal of Public Health, 83*(4), 491–492.

Thompson, D. (1990, January 22). The AIDS political machine. *Time*, pp. 24–25.

Wermick, A. (1991). *Promotional culture: Advertising, ideology, and symbolic expression*. Newbury Park, CA: Sage.

CHAPTER TEN

The Monet Exhibit

Today corporations often help make an art museum's collections more accessible to the public. The bottom line is a good reputation for the company and more visitors for the art museum.

The leading European clothes designer Yves Saint Laurent funds music in Brooklyn and films in Cape Town (Weber, 1998). Designer Hugo Boss has entered the lifeblood of the Guggenheim Museum in four European countries. Pierre Berge, a Yves Saint Laurent executive, denies that public relations is the goal of their involvement. However, one could argue that association with the art world does foster a good name for a company. Selling clothes is much like selling art. In fact, Cowen (1998) noted that art has always been associated with the market.

In 1998 Boston's Fleet Bank decided to underwrite the Monet exhibit at Boston's Museum of Fine Arts (MFA). The exhibit was the biggest ever held at the museum. The exhibit also received the largest amount of money ever provided for a MFA exhibit from corporate sponsorship.[1] This Monet show became the largest collection of his late paintings ever assembled for exhibit. In addition, the number of visitors to the museum was greater than for any previous MFA exhibit.

The public relations campaign for the Monet exhibit facilitated the public response. The Monet exhibit ran from September to December 1998, but the campaign began several months earlier.

The question to be answered in this chapter is: How did the museum's public relations campaign represent Monet to the public? Framing is a useful paradigm to examine the construction of any public relations message (Hallahan, 1999).

The public relations material in the Monet exhibit campaign tapped into the semiotic world of the art consumer, especially the reader of the Sunday *Boston Globe* newsmagazine, in which an important story about the exhibit appeared a week before the exhibit opened. Words and images were used in the story that were already part of the experience of the potential visitor to the exhibit. Thus, the public relations for the exhibit became an example of using the symbolic world of the consumer to sell the exhibit. Monet was represented as the most important artist of the twentieth century, and this exhibit was represented as a must-see for every art lover.

This chapter examines the relationship between art as commodity and public relations practice as product promotion. The goal is to deconstruct a public relations text. The museum had a product, the Monet exhibit, and its campaign to promote Monet went into action several months before the opening.

To deconstruct public relations is not simply to question public relations, but rather to examine its practice, its text, and its discourse, which is a material cultural artifact. This chapter raises questions about how the Monet exhibit was represented as a public relations text.

The significance of the problem and the justification for investigating it rests on the importance of looking at public relations practice from a critical perspective. Also, it is important to examine the relationship between culture and art. The feasibility of doing the proposed study is possible because the MFA has made available its public relations campaign strategies for the Monet exhibit.[2]

Marchand (1998) discussed how public relations helped build the business for many corporations through creating imagery in words and pictures for the consumer. He traced several important campaigns in the history of this country, including the Pennsylvania Railroad and AT&T. A modern business, like a museum, cannot exist without the work of public relations to create an image that generates acceptance among the public.

Bayley (1989) analyzed the relationship between art and commerce. He noted that museums were born in the nineteenth century, at the same time as department stores. Both sell goods to the consumer; both need to be represented to the public. Therefore, one might say that art by its nature needs the market to exist and become "art." Bayley contended that, at one time, commerce and culture were one.

According to Cowen (1998), the market drives the work of the artist. Culture is based on the business acumen of the artist or those who promote him/her. Cowen showed how painting in the Renaissance was the business of selling art rather than doing art. The masterpieces of art came about for all to enjoy today because a king, a bishop, or a merchant requested the painting from an artist. In contrast, the Dutch painters usually made the painting first and marketed it afterwards to a general buyership. In latter times, growing markets in music, literature, and fine arts have moved creators away from dependence on patronage. The Renaissance, the Enlightenment, the nineteenth-century romantic movement, and twentieth-century modernism all brought art further into the market sphere. In nineteenth-century France Impressionist painting prospered only once its makers established their own independent networks of marketing and distribution.

Cultural studies literature dealing with the media sometimes takes the view that the consumer is completely gullible, and the critics, therefore, must protect the consumer. However, cultural studies writers like Stuart Hall think that the consumer is quite capable of using popular culture for his/her own needs, no matter what the critic may say. Therefore, the reader can even read a meaning from the text that is against what the producer wanted or intended.

Urstadt (1999) discussed how Volvo invited a group of journalists to a lodge out West for an all-expenses-paid weekend. During the weekend each journalist had the opportunity to drive a new Volvo. Urstadt noted that this is the way media relations with big companies works today. The public relations professional markets to the writer, who will devote to the product or service an article that hopefully endorses the product. The product is thus framed as news.

We are defining public relations as the managing of information to a specific public to support a company's product or service. In that definition the assumption is that the capitalist system is well and alive. On the other hand, popular culture critics like the Frankfurt School take the position that corporate America dictates the taste and desires to the rest of the country.

The consumer can, however, make up his/her own mind about a product or a service. People will be more likely to attend a well-promoted film, for example, but that alone will not make the film a success—only the box office receipts can do the job. If people like the film, they will go to it, pay their money, and get something out of it. The notion that media cannot be criticized if audiences enjoy them simply replaces elitism with populism (Currie, 1997).

Promotional materials, as found in such forms as public relations, provide a research area to investigate the relationship between language and culture. This chapter deconstructs a public relations campaign to promote an art exhibit.

Dufur (1997) discussed representation of African American athletes in advertising. Through content analysis, he showed that the message is that African American athletes' success comes from physical abilities rather than hard work, intelligence, or leadership.

McFall (1998) noted that economic practices are culturally defined, whereas cultural meanings are shared through economic activities in every society. The power of representation in public relations, marketing, and advertising therefore becomes critical in thinking about what is important in the culture.

Tsao (1997) found that vagueness was a major characteristic of drug information provided in television drug commercials.

Alaniz and Wilkes (1995) discussed the critical issue of meanings and values that are established, reinforced, transmitted, and absorbed into popular culture as a result of advertising to the Mexican American community. Cultural components are appropriated, refigured, and resold to consumers in a commodity form. Promotional language is thus structured according to the needs of the market.

One can examine the semiology of the promotion of a product by deconstructing both historical fact and the cultural images deriving from that historical experience (Alaniz & Wilkes, 1995). Public relations invites the active participation of audiences. At the very least, it invites the gaze of viewers who bring these new symbolic systems to consciousness. Most commonly, viewers actively participate in the mixing of these signs, thus becoming part of the sign system themselves, essential components in the process of creating meaning.

Public relations is the process of producing symbolic material in word and image to motivate a particular public to take action. The fact that the practice is concerned with language makes the study of public relations discourse important. Framing of that discourse is one way to discuss public relations.

Hallahan (1999) viewed framing as a strategic public relations process. Framing is a critical activity in the construction of social reality, because it helps shape the perspectives through which people see the world. Hallahan maintained that framing is not merely useful but essential to public relations. In developing programs, public relations professionals fundamentally operate as *frame strategists*. Hallahan argued that it is important to research how "information" from the public relations source becomes news. The study of public relations as a source in news framing has been largely overlooked, even though Hallahan showed that much of the news we see and hear every day is generated by public relations work. He concluded by noting that framing is a potentially useful paradigm to examine public relations.

Although Hallahan discussed framing, he didn't lay out a methodology to explore it. He proposed an understanding of the concept of framing as essential in public relations. Finally, he suggested that the public relations field would benefit from additional research that builds on and extends the concept of framing. The question becomes, then, one of looking at an appropriate method to examine framing in action in a real public relations situation.

Thibault (1991) employed semiotics to propose an interdisciplinary method for both the social sciences and the humanities. Thus, the analysis of culturally constituted sign systems is grounded in the context of social action. The reader encounters the text from within a particular social experience, and the encounter itself is a social experience. A person reads as a member of some social group that shares common bonds: family, friends, political affiliation, employment, residence. All create commonality for the reader.

Context of the signs allows the reader to make sense of the signs. Textual meanings are made in and through specific socially and historically contingent meaning-making practices, which enact specific systems of foregrounded meaning relations.

Mortelmans (1997) discussed advertising from a social semiotic approach to illustrate the symbolic representation of luxury. A Sunday newspaper magazine, like an advertisement, can also be treated as a text or an aggregate of signs. Mortelmans argued that semiotic analysis relies too often on the individual capacities of the analyst to go find hidden myths or deeper layers of meaning in a text like an advertisement. It is important to overcome such criticism.

The object of a semiotic analysis is a "text." Analysis of a text requires the systematic breaking down or deconstruction of the codes (structures, rules) in order to determine the fundamental structures that produce a meaning. The "interpretation" or "reading" of the text is actually not the deconstruction of it, but rather the reconstruction that produces another text or "parallel" text (e.g., the critic's review).

Rejection of the creator's intent is important. The focus is on the text as it appears in the media. In this study, the text is a media product as a representation of public relations practice.

Three steps proposed by Mortelmans are followed in the analysis of two public relations pieces: a news story and an ad for the Monet exhibit. First is the description of the text, which can include the layout, number of pages, print versus pictures, color or black-and-white photos, and so on. Second is the analysis of the text to disclose its so-called manifest information. Third is the interpretation of the text from the context in which it appears. This is where the concept of *framing* becomes most important. It is here, for example, that we give the text its meaning of news or entertainment. It flows from the description and the manifest information presented.

The campaign materials could be viewed from a semiotic approach, which would give a method to framing the story as news. The text here is a *Boston Globe* magazine news story on Monet. The objective of the analysis is to describe the framing process for the Monet exhibit as news.

Using Mortelmans' three-step process, the text—the *Boston Globe* of September 13, 1998—is examined. The exhibit of Monet's early twentieth-century work, the largest collection of his work to be displayed, opened 1 week later, on September 20, 1998.

The *Boston Globe Magazine* for Sunday, September 13, 1998, had a cover with a large color reproduction of the Monet painting *Houses of Parliament, Sunset*, painted in London in 1904. These words appeared below the 8 × 8½-inch reproduction: "The Modern Monet. A Museum of Fine Arts show of the painter's late works offers a rare chance to see the 20th century through Impressionist eyes."

The article, which began on page 16, covered 16 pages and included 7 color reproductions of Monet's paintings and 2 black-and-white photos. The story was written by one of the paper's staff journalists.

On page 6 there was a Fleet Bank ad for the exhibit. A large color reproduction of Monet's *Water Lilies* (1907) was part of the ad. This was not one of the paintings included in the story about the Monet exhibit. The words in the ad were: "A 20th century master. Brought to you by a 21st century bank."

The story itself reads like a journal of the writer's trip to London, Venice, Paris, and Giverny—all cities in which Monet painted the works included in the MFA exhibit. Often, the writer wrote of her experiences with the personal *I* as she traced the route that Monet took in painting the works that were featured in the exhibit.

In a lecture to representatives of the Public Relations of Society of America, on Monday, October 19, 1998 in Boston, the Museum of Fine Arts Public Relations Director outlined the public relations campaign. There were several strategies. In March 1998, with the sponsorship of Fleet, the MFA held a press event at a New York French restaurant with more than 70 national press members attending. In May of that year, a European press tour was conducted that traced Monet's travel through London, Venice, Paris, and Giverny. In June and July, there was an outreach to U.S. dailies that included all sections and travel supplements. Part of this effort was a visit to key members of the New York press. In August, photo opportunities and a visit from the French Counsel were available. The press preview for the exhibit was 10 days before the opening. The press kit had 25 releases, including a "top 10."

One of the results of the campaign strategy from the May trip to Europe was a story in the September 13th issue of the *Boston Globe*.[3] However, to the reader it was not an obvious advertisement of the exhibit. Thus, it was quite different from Fleet Bank's ad on page 6.

The placement of the story is in the context of news. The experience of the reader tells him/her that this is not advertising, but instead is legitimate news. The reader knows the difference between an ad and a news story, and thus decodes this public relations piece as news.

The placement of the story, the size of type for the story, the inclusion of the writer's byline, the objectivity of the information presented, and the dominance of a headline for the story are all cultural codes for the production of this text as news. Through "good" public relations, the Monet exhibit was thus framed as news.

The *Globe* editorial staff thought a piece about Monet and the museum exhibit would "sell," and therefore chose to run it in the coveted magazine section of the Sunday paper. The selling of the exhibit through the placement of the news story (feature) about the exhibit continues the tradition of marketing art. Also, the importance that art takes in the culture is largely structured by the market for the artwork. The *Globe* showed that there is much interest among its readers in Monet.

The *Globe* was involved in what Hallahan (1999) called *frame negotiation*—an exchange between the media outlet and a public relations source that generates the story idea for such a frame. The story appeared as a news story in the newspaper and thus was framed as news. The reader saw the story as a well-researched feature that promoted the Monet exhibit, but was unaware of the public relations strategy behind the placement of the story. The appearance of the story in the *Globe* was not by accident, but rather was a planned strategy on the part of the MFA public relations team to promote the exhibit. That was also the case with many of the other local and national stories about the exhibit.

No matter what the MFA public relations team wanted, it was the decision of the newspaper to run the story as news, and thus the newspaper framed a public relations text as news. In that action, the paper marketed Monet. Thus, we see culture as art represented in the exhibit story. The story sold Monet, but also sold MFA public relations practice to the reader.

This chapter set out to show public relations framing as a way to sell to the culture a product that already had a market willing to accept it. Hallahan (1999) asserted that the central idea in framing is contextualization. Framing, he said, puts information into a context and establishes frames of reference so people can evaluate information, comprehend meanings, and take action if appropriate.

Monet was, arguably, the most popular painter in the twentieth century. The Boston Museum of Fine Arts sold the story idea about the Monet exhibit to the *Boston Globe* perhaps because the culture already had a strong acceptance of this artist. That may also have influenced the MFA's decision to sponsor the exhibit in the first place. It illustrates the economic relationship between art and culture.

To deconstruct public relations is to place the campaign within the context in which it is produced, read, and hopefully accepted. The Monet story in the *Boston Globe* was a public relations text read as a news story, not as advertising. It was framed to the reader as objective news, not as advertising. The ad by Fleet Bank, on the other hand, was framed as an ad although directed to the same reader.

At the same time as we see the importance of public relations for commerce in the culture, we see that art depends on commerce for its survival in the culture. They are intimately connected.

This chapter was an example of researching the relationship between art and culture, specifically the representation of art in a public relations campaign. Because public relations itself is a construction, its practice needs to be open to critical inquiry.

The limitation of this project is that only one part of the MFA public relations campaign—placement of the *Boston Globe* story—was examined. Perhaps future research might look at more of the campaign as other expressions of framing.

REFERENCES

Alaniz, M., & Wilkes, C. (1995). Reinterpreting Latino culture in the commodity form: The case of alcohol advertising in the Mexican American community. *Hispanic Journal of Behavioral Sciences, 17*(4), 430–451.

Bayley, S. (1989). *Commerce and culture: From pre-industrial art to post-industrial value*. London: Design Museum (published in association with Fourth Estate).

Cowen, T. (1998). *In praise of commercial culture*. Cambridge, MA: Harvard University Press.

Currie, D. (1997). Decoding femininity: Advertisements and their teenage readers. *Gender and Society, 11*(4), 453–475.
Dufur, M. (1997). Race logic and "being like Mike": Representations of athletes in advertising, 1985–1994. *Sociological Focus, 30*(4), 345–356.
Hallahan, K. (1999). Seven models of framing: Implications for public relations. *Journal of Public Relations Research, 11*(3), 205–242.
Marchand, R. (1998). *Creating the corporate soul: The rise of public relations and corporate imagery in American big business*. Berkeley: University of California Press.
McFall, E. (1998). *Towards an ethnographic study of advertising practice*. Paper presented at the International Sociological Association meeting.
Mortelmans, D. (1997). Visual representation of luxury: An analysis of print advertisements for jewelry. *Communications, 22*(1), 69–91.
Thibault, P. (1991). *Social semiotics as praxis: Text, social meaning making, and Nabokov's Ada*. Minneapolis: University of Minnesota Press.
Tsao, J. (1997). Informational and symbolic content of over-the-counter drug advertising on television. *Journal of Drug Education, 27*(2), 173–197.
Urstadt, B. (1999). Dipping extremely low in the lap of corporate luxury: A sell-out's tale. *The Baffler, 12*, 47–60.
Weber, N. F. (1998, Fall). Haute giving. *The American Benefactor*, pp. 74–78.

ENDNOTES

[1]The total given by Fleet Bank was $1.2 million, which was the largest donation in the history of the Museum of Fine Arts, according to the director of public relations for the MFA. (Lecture by Dawn Griffin, public relations director for the MFA, at the Public Relations Society of America annual meeting, Boston, Monday, October 18, 1998.)
[2]Ibid.
[3]Ibid.

CHAPTER ELEVEN

Olympic Gold

A critical view of public relations has become a part of the growing body of public relations theory (Berger, 1999; Elwood, 1995; L'Etang & Pieczka, 1996; Toth & Heath, 1992). Therefore, the more common empirical and behavioral view of public relations is not as dominant. The same paradigm shift has already taken place in the field of mass communication research and theory (Hall, 1980).

A critical view of public relations shows a movement toward "understanding" public relations rather than predicting behavior through public relations activities. Such an understanding has been borrowed from the humanities, in particular from such areas as philosophy and literary criticism. Altman's work on the Better Homes in America campaign of the 1920s is an example of such critical research work in the area of public relations theory. She noted, "The meaning of work for boys and girls, men and women was constituted in the discourse [of the campaign]" (Altman, 1990, p. 298).

One important school of thought in literary criticism is semiotics, whose concern is the context and structure of signs or symbols rather than the effect or influence of the piece on the audience members. Such a view of writing sees language (also called *discourse*) as a way to understand the organization and the culture, rather than as a tool for behavioral change. Hawkes (1977) pointed that out in his work on semiotics when he argued: "Once a 'science of signs' has demonstrated that the sign-system of writing does NOT act simply as a transparent window onto an established 'reality,' it can be identified as a sign-system in its own right, with its own properties and its own distinct character" (p. 146).

This chapter seeks to discuss the role of public relations language in establishing the power elite, meaning, and ideology. The route taken here is one of looking at semiotics and how it views writing, especially from the work of French philosopher Jacques Derrida. The method is to deconstruct a U.S. national public relations campaign text.

The future of research in mass communication as well as public relations will be looking at the issue of "discourse" more and more (see Hall, 1980). An article by Van Dijk (1990) predicts that kind of research. He noted:

> Mass communication research has a long tradition of content analytical approaches to media messages. Occasionally, linguistic studies about the grammatical features of media language have been carried out. Few detailed discourse analyses of media genres (mostly news and advertising) have been made during the last two decades, and we may therefore expect that the 1990s will show an enhanced attention, both in discourse analysis and in mass communication research, for the subtle details of mass media genres. Such analyses should not be limited to pure "structural" studies, but must also pay attention to the links between media message structures, on the one hand, and the micro sociology and cognitive psychology of news production, reading the uses by readers or viewers, or the broader economic, political, societal, cultural or ideological contexts of news, advertising of their institutional contexts, on the other. (p. 152)

Van Dijk's prediction has come true since today we see more critical studies of public relations dealing with discourse.

He implied a greater use of a critical and semiotic view of public communication. One important early work of discourse analysis on the topic of advertising was by Williamson (1980). She treated ads as ways of creating identity in a culture. The consumer finds his/her meaning in a particular ad. The ads work by an exchange of signs, and an enmeshing of the subjects in that exchange: A process concealed by the participation of the "active subject" (Williamson, p. 167).

The purpose of this chapter is not to discuss the vast field of semiotics, but simply to show how some insights from this field might help us understand public relations writing. We do not get into the differences between the French and Anglo/American semiotics tradition. That would take us far afield for our purposes here. There are books and articles one can consult for such a treatment (e.g., Silverman, 1983).

Semiotics looks at the sign, the signified, and the signification (code) on two levels. The first level one might call the *cultural definition*, and the other is the *myth* behind that definition. For example, a word (sign) represents something (signified) for the person because it is a part of a larger system or code (signification). The sign cannot be understood apart from its link to the code or larger system. Therefore, in the case of writing, the writer and the reader understand the word (sign) in the context of their signification for a particular culture. The writer must use the prevailing signs of the culture as his/her way of constituting being in the culture. At the same time, the reader understands the written piece and thereby his/her own existence in the culture by using and understanding those signs himself/herself.

To understand writing from the semiotic view is to address the issue of meaning within a particular cultural context. Words are not simply vehicles to express thought—they create the culture and its ideology. The sign in relationship with other signs creates the meaning for both the producer and the consumer of the message.

Derrida made an important distinction: *difference* (in English, *differentiation*) and *differance* (a deferment, in English; Derrida, 1978). Derrida's theory of deconstruction breaks with all traditional, normative ideas of textual commentary and critique. It is not so much interested in what the text says—what it is "about" at the express thematic level—as in the organization of its logical resources *despite* or *against* its manifest drift (Norris, 1987).

Language is a structuring process. Words do not simply show differences; they also structure them in a type of ordering (e.g., where someone is superior, another inferior, and a third might be equal). We see in the choice of words an ordering, apart from the express theme of the material.

At the same time, the written work lives its own life within both the reader and the writer in what Gadamer called the *herme-*

neutic triangle (Mickey, 1990). The symbol or word becomes the way we understand ourselves and our culture; it is not something we use, but rather something that uses us. We dialogue with the word. We are born in the word.

The language we use creates a certain ideology in the process. We accept the language and, therefore, accept the ideology. Derrida's deconstruction points to the chains with which language binds us. Thus, the basic need to become self-critical is our only survival tool. Language is the skin that enables us to encounter the world. As with our own skin, its power is taken for granted in acting in the world.

In his media research Hall gave an excellent example of how the taken-for-grantedness of the language we use in public communication incorporates an ideology. He wrote:

> A statement like "the strike of Leyland tool-makers today further weakened Britain's economic position" was premised on a whole set of taken-for-granted propositions about how the economy worked, what the national interest was, and so on. For it to win credibility, the whole logic of capitalist production had to be assumed to be true. Much the same could be said about any item in a conventional news bulletin [read also "news release"], that, without a whole range of unstated premises or pieces of taken-for-granted knowledge about the world, each descriptive statement would be literally unintelligible. But this "deep structure" of presuppositions, which made the statement ideologically "grammatical," were rarely made explicit and were largely unconscious, either to those who deployed them (writers) to make sense of the world or to those who were required to make sense of it (reader). (Hall, 1980, p. 74)

Semiotics calls us to look at the context in which we write and the context in which we read. To become aware of the language that we "use" is to become aware of ourselves and our relationships with other persons and the world. A critical view such as semiotics enables us to see ourselves as products of a particular culture. Silverman noted, "The discourse within which the subject finds its identity is always the discourse of the other—of a symbolic order which transcends the subject, and which orchestrates its entire history" (Silverman, 1983, p. 194).

Language is a form of creating empowerment, not simply a way of getting the message to another. By our choice of words, we show a structure in which an elite is created and a dominated class is subjugated. The relationship is not simply expressed in language, but, indeed, language establishes the relationship. We are not talking about hidden meanings of a text, but rather the structures the text employs to establish its case. The writer employs a certain language that *is* the culture, and the reader becomes part of that culture in the language.

Public relations seeks to influence constituencies through various communication strategies (Wilcox, Ault, & Agee, 1989). One of the most important strategies is writing. When we view writing as a strategy, public relations is perceived as a vehicle to behavioral change. Such a view of communication has a positivist and empirical slant. Communication effectiveness is therefore measured by its ability to achieve a measurable impact on a significant public or target audience.

The intention of this chapter is to look at public relations from a critical and more humanistic framework. Rather than seeing writing as a tool to get a message out there, we want to look at it as a way of establishing relationships, identity, cultural solidarity, and, in the process, a dominant ideology.

Our way to do that is to take the perspective of semiotics, which seeks to look at signs as a way of codification or creating myth in a society. Language is not getting a message out there, but instead is a means of understanding self and the world.

What we do is look at a press release generated by the Miller High Life Brewing Company in the summer of 1990. The subject of the release is the 1992 Olympics. Here is the lead: "Olympians Jackie Joyner-Kersee, Dan Jansen and Quinn Buckner will serve as spokespeople for Miller Brewing Company's nationwide fundraising program to raise $1 million to benefit the U.S. Olympic Training Centers."

We use the three assumptions presented by Trenhold (1991) in her summary of semiotics to discuss the release. Any words in quotation marks in the following discussion come from the actual text of the press release. Trenhold's first assumption was that language and other semiotic codes are self-contained systems of differences. In this question, we are looking for contrasts or differences highlighted in the language used. As one of the largest breweries in the country, we might say first that "Miller" represented the beer industry. Miller was helping to support Olympic training, in contrast to nonsupport from government and other private sources.

This was a "new" 3-year sponsoring "relationship" between Miller and the Olympic Training Centers. Miller was indicating that any prior relationship was now replaced by this one. It was to continue for a period of time: 3 years. An organization took its role as a "relationship" with the Olympic hopefuls. What if some didn't want the relationship? It existed nonetheless.

The fundraising campaign was to help "buy" training time for America's Olympic hopefuls. Time is a commodity that can be purchased by corporations. Corporations wield a godlike power of providing time for the consumer. The release read: "The contributions will help provide training time for American athletes."

The Olympic "dream" was referred to several times. Many young people hope to get to the Olympics; therefore, it is a dream for them. Whether or not it becomes a reality is open to question. Miller gave itself the role of dream-provider in this language.

Trenhold's second assumption was that meaning is created not by individuals, but instead by the discourses that surround and constitute them. Sign systems are not individual, but instead social constructions. Signifying systems exist because groups of people agree to use them. Just as there are different groups of language users, so there are many different ways of signifying that are called *discourse*.

The discourse of the Miller Brewing Company was the discourse of corporate America: It finds its meaning in philanthropic work, and, in this case, helping the Olympics.

Good public relations strategy dictates that Miller needed to publicly say what it was doing to give something back to the nation. That something was leading a fundraising effort across the nation for the Olympic Training Centers. Miller, as a national company, needed to focus its effort on what the nation could identify with as its own. The nation sees the Olympics as expressive of international cooperation, wholesome athletic competition, and national pride. Therefore, the choice of the Olympics as its philanthropic tool gave Miller an international visibility as well.

The international meaning is that big business supports the Olympics in this country, where capitalism makes everything happen. Therefore, one might say Miller's involvement in the Olympics was capitalism. Capitalism is the American way. It is America.

Trenhold's third assumption was that to understand communication, it is necessary to uncover the latent ideological meanings hidden beneath communication's surface. By its campaign to raise money for the Olympics the ideology Miller made clear is that sports is linked to the buying and selling of alcohol. The Olympics—where the youngest, brightest, most talented athletes gather—is connected with alcohol. Also, the alcohol industry in this country has a great deal of clout by the mere fact that it *can* align itself with the Olympics.

Most people are simply not aware that when they use a particular discourse they are accepting a value system; that no act of communication is apolitical. Language, as Derrida pointed out, is not simply differences but a structure of power: superior and inferior. Here, the Olympics are indebted to the beer industry.

Therefore, in communicating in this campaign, Miller was not simply expressing its concern about the young people who wanted to be part of the Olympics. In that discourse Miller established its capitalism and a strong link between alcohol and sports. At the same time, the consumer public saw—and therefore accepted—Miller as the champion of the Olympics.

Language creates the relationship. The structure of power becomes real in the words: "support" from Miller and "acceptance" on the part of the Olympic organization and the readers, listeners, and viewers of this information from Miller's news release. The language assumes a certain taken-for-grantedness from both the writer and the reader.

This semiotic view of public relations writing is important for understanding how language interacts with the culture by creating a power through an accepted and unquestioned ideology for that culture. Such has been the purpose of this chapter: to argue for a critical view of public relations writing. By *critical* is meant a look at the structure, myth, and relationships within the language used.

Finally, this chapter was not intended to suggest that Miller should have disenfranchised itself from the Olympics, but instead simply to argue how public relations discourse creates meaning for individuals within the culture and for the culture itself. However, that meaning is not apolitical. Shapiro wrote: "A failure to exercise a literary self-consciousness amounts to the adoption of a depoliticizing posture, the acceptance of institutional imperatives" (Shapiro, 1984, p. 239).

REFERENCES

Altman, K. (1990). Consuming ideology: The better homes in America campaign. *Critical Studies in Mass Communication, 7*, 286–307.

Berger, B. K. (1999). The Halicon affair: Public relations and the construction of ideological world view. *Journal of Public Relations Research, 11*(3), 187–203.

Derrida, J. (1978). *Writing and difference* (Alan Bass, Trans.). Chicago: University of Chicago Press.

Elwood, W. (Ed.). (1995). *Public relations inquiry and rhetorical criticism*. Westport, CT: Praeger.

Hall, S. (1980). *Culture, society and media*. London: Hutchinson.

Hawkes, T. (1977). *Structuralism and semiotics*. Berkeley: University of California Press.

L'Etang, J., & Pieczka, M. (Eds.). (1996). *Critical perspectives in public relations*. London: International Thomson Business Press.

Mickey, T. (1990, June). *Hermeneutics and public relations writing: Understanding the text*. Paper presented at the annual meeting of the International Communication Association (ICA), Dublin, Ireland.

Norris, C. (1987). *Derrida*. Cambridge, MA: Harvard University Press.

Shapiro, M. (1984). Literacy production as a politicizing practice. In M. Shapiro (Ed.), *Language and politics* (pp. 215–253). New York: New York University Press.

Silverman, K. (1983). *The subject of semiotics*. New York: Oxford University Press.

Toth, E., & Heath, R. (Eds.). (1992). *Rhetorical and critical approaches to public relations*. Hillsdale, NJ: Lawrence Erlbaum Associates.

Trenhold, S. (1991). *Human communication theory*. Englewood Cliffs, NJ: Prentice-Hall.

Van Dijk, T. A. (1990). The future of the field: Discourse analysis in the 1990s. *Text, 10*, 133–156.

Wilcox, D. L., Ault, P., & Agee, W. (1989). *Public relations strategies and tactics* (2nd ed.). New York: Harper & Row.

Williamson, J. (1980). *Decoding advertisements: Ideology and meaning in advertising*. London: Marion Boyars.

About the Author

Thomas J. Mickey is a Professor of Communication Studies at Bridgewater State College in Bridgewater, MA where he teaches public relations and public relations writing. He also directs students in the public relations internships. Mickey teaches part-time at U Mass Boston and Boston University.

He has written one book, *Sociodrama: An Interpretive Theory for the Practice of Public Relations*. He has had several articles published in the academic journal *Public Relations Review*. During the last few years he has presented papers at several national and international conferences including the Ethics and Technology Conference in Chicago, the National Communication Association annual meeting in New York, the International Public Relations Research Conference in College Park, MD, and the Public Relations Society of America annual meeting in Nashville.

Before coming to Bridgewater while he taught at New England College in Henniker, NH Mickey was a member of Yankee Public Relations Society of America where he served on several committees including Professional Development. He is a member of Boston's PRSA where he has served on the Board as well as on some of the group's committees.

Author Index

R

S

T

U

V

W

Subject Index